Picturing Corporate Practice

Jay A. Mitchell

Professor of Law
Director, Organizations and Transactions Clinic
Stanford Law School

WEST
ACADEMIC
PUBLISHING

© 2016 LEG, Inc. d/b/a West Academic
        444 Cedar Street, Suite 700
        St. Paul, MN 55101
        1-877-888-1330

West, West Academic Publishing, and West Academic
are trademarks of West Publishing Corporation, used
under license.

Printed in the United States of America

ISBN: 978-1-63460-464-2

to Kim, Laura, and Sarah

Contents

Introduction

Corporate lawyers do basically two things.

First, we look at situations and offer our thoughts. A client seeks advice; we study the problem and report back. Second, we create plans (for a transaction, or a new corporate structure) and then help document and carry out the plan. In each case, we facilitate decision-making about complex situations, and we create tangible products that reflect and implement the decisions. In each case, we help clients get from (current) state A to (better) state B.

This isn't easy to do. It's not obvious how to get started on a project. Or to plan a deal. Nor is it always clear what to create for the client in response to a problem or goal, or how to get going on building it. The materials we encounter, such as big contracts and disclosure documents, can be pretty daunting, too. And the practice itself can be somewhat mysterious. Corporate work, with its collaborative- and business-oriented character, is rather different from the contentiousness and caselaw of litigation familiar to law students.

This book is intended for lawyers new to the practice and law students interested in corporate work. It's designed to help folks get their hands around the job. The book offers some ways of thinking about the work and provides practical suggestions for doing it, with plenty of how-things-work information and vocabulary along the way.

How This Book is Organized

The book is organized as follows:

Chapter 1 offers several broad observations about corporate practice, including overviews of the core activities of advice development and transaction management, and about the products we create for our clients.

Chapter 2 is about visual communication as a basic tool for corporate lawyers. You may not have talked about it much in school, but making a diagram, timeline, or simple sketch can be an exceedingly useful exercise in helping you get a grip on a problem, plan, or document.

Chapter 3 offers a step-by-step approach to situation analysis and advice development, the fundamental lawyer work of breaking down situations and then building them back up in a methodical but imaginative way.

Chapter 4 is about transaction planning and execution. It steps through multiple factors considered in developing a transaction plan, discusses due diligence, closings, and deal documents, and suggests some practical tools for carrying out the project management tasks at the center of deal practice. There's a fair amount of vocabulary in this chapter.

Chapter 5 introduces legal documents, the basic products of the trade. The discussion considers, among other things, the business orientation and common sense of legal documents, and introduces standard components, organizational schemes, and conventions of contracts and other legal materials. There's vocabulary here, too.

Chapter 6 is about reading and creating legal documents. It offers ideas for dealing with big documents, and for drafting them. The chapter suggests ways to help you see the many things you need to see in legal documents, and discusses everyday activities such as use of models, dealing with comments, and proofreading.

Chapter 7 concerns meetings of corporate boards. Board meetings are a common example of advisory, deal, and document work coming together, and a nice example of how our work often centers on process design. The chapter discusses meeting preparation and outcome documentation through minutes and resolutions.

Chapter 8 contains some observations about litigation. We corporate lawyers decided not to be litigators, and the vast majority of situations don't turn sour. But we still need to be mindful, in our advisory and document work, of the possibility of litigation. The chapter offers several suggestions about litigation anticipation and touches on attorney-client privilege considerations in corporate practice.

Chapter 9 discusses disclosure documents filed by public companies with the Securities and Exchange Commission. Lawyers in all sorts of practices regularly encounter such documents, and it's just good to know your way around them. More broadly, SEC filings are great tools for learning about business, and corporate lawyers should always be learning about business. There's a lot of vocabulary in this chapter.

Chapter 10 is about working with nonprofit organizations, the typical client in a pro bono engagement. Corporate lawyers are well-suited for pro bono work, the engagements can be quite challenging, and we can do a lot of good. The discussion includes sector-specific vocabulary.

Chapter 11 is about clients. Clients have really tough jobs. The chapter offers a brief portrait of client life and a number of practical

ideas for how we can help them out through our homework, communications (including especially e-mails), and personal interactions.

In essence, Chapter 1 is a short, high-level discussion, Chapters 2–8 center on orientation and practical ideas, Chapters 9–10 provide useful background information, and Chapter 11 winds it up with why we're here in the first place: to serve our clients.

The book includes a number of diagrams and other illustrations. Some — especially those in the advice, deal work, and documents chapters — are suggestive of things you might try in practice. Others are intended to reinforce and complement the text. None are the right or only way to draw legal pictures; indeed, a central message of the visual communication discussion is that there is no right way to do it. What matters is what works for you.

A terminology note: the book uses the term "corporate" in two ways in describing the practice. In most uses (such as the title), the term refers to business and transactional practice generally. In some cases, the book distinguishes between "corporate" work (such as mergers and acquisitions) and "commercial" work (such as licensing). The meaning should be clear from the context.

The text also includes call-outs of work by several practitioners and scholars; source information is presented at the end of the book.

A Final Note Before We Get Started

Let's be honest. Legal practice can be a grind at times. You dig through due diligence materials, work through draft after draft of a single paragraph, cross-check against technical filing requirements, proofread giant contracts, chase signatures, organize phone calls, and deal with endless e-mails.

That's all just reality. These things are part of the job, and you to have to do them really well.

The ways of thinking about the work offered here are intended to give you a broader context and frame for these activities; the deal planning and board meeting discussions are examples.

The practical suggestions, such as the encouragements to make little drawings or the proofreading checklist in chapter 6, are intended to help you with both core analytical, planning, and writing work and with the attention-to-detail and execution stuff that's really important in a job centered on getting products and projects completed on time and at a very high quality level.

The discussions here are also intended to suggest the intellectual and professional enjoyment you can have along the way.

It's quite gratifying to look at messy situations, get a handle on the problem, come up with a practical solution, and help the client rest easier about things.

It's challenging, engaging, and exciting to steer a complex transaction through multiple constraints under meaningful time pressure, and to get it closed for the client.

It's satisfying to pick up a big contract, know where to look and what's going on, quickly imagine implications, and identify 50 ways to make it better.

And it's neat to start with some general ideas, sketch out a plan, and end up with a set of integrated and polished pieces of writing used and appreciated by the client.

Thinking about all of this as a craft, where we use tools and build useful objects for our clients to help them build their businesses, is a good way to think about it. It's fun to fix problems and make high-quality products that help people out.

Good luck — and have fun out there.

1 / Observations about the Practice

Corporate work can be unfamiliar to law students and new lawyers. This chapter offers several broad observations about the practice and some ways to think about it.

Let's first deal with the litigation comparison.

Corporate work is different than litigation in that corporate is largely collaborative in nature. We're usually trying to put something together with another party, rather than fighting with them. Oftentimes there is no opposing party; it's just the client and us. We generally write for regular people, not lawyers and judges. And we spend more time dealing with business facts than we do legal doctrine.

This chapter offers some high-level observations about the practice in anticipation of fuller discussions later in the book. As we'll see, corporate lawyers work at both the entity level of an organization (on things like mergers) and deep in the operations of individual business units (on things like marketing practices). We give advice about both internal matters (for

example, corporate governance) and external matters (financial disclosure). And of course we help clients plan and execute transactions, from raising capital to acquiring real estate.

In doing that work, we devote considerable time to reading and writing all sorts of legal documents, and we need to, because there's a lot going on in legal documents. We're calendar-focused, given the nature of deal work and the fact that our clients operate in line with multiple commercial and other timeframes. And we bounce around between big picture and little picture considerations, from studying brand strategy to looking for typos.

Lots of business, lots of documents, lots of project management and execution.

Let's get started.

Corporate vs. Commercial

Our work falls into two broad categories.

Corporate work occurs at the organizational level. It involves dealing with the entity: structure, governance, financing and so on. Practice areas include corporate governance, securities, corporate finance, and mergers and acquisitions.

Corporate lawyers spend considerable time with state law corporations statutes and the federal securities laws. They interact with boards of directors, senior executives, investment bankers, commercial banks, accountants, investors, and regulators.

Commercial work, on the other hand, occurs at the operations level. It involves dealing with the core business: product development, procurement, distribution, licensing, marketing, sales. The great variety of business models, products, and services in the marketplace means there is great variety in the legal work.

Commercial lawyers work with intellectual property, antitrust, data privacy, contract, consumer protection, and lots of other areas of law. They may deal with complex regulatory regimes such as those relating to pharmaceuticals or telecommunications. They interact not so much with bankers but instead with people in the business: engineers, scientists, product managers, merchandisers, marketers, account reps, sales teams.

Both corporate and commercial lawyers give advice and plan and carry out deals.

Advice

We give advice about all sorts of things.

We get lots of questions from clients. They may want to know if a contract permits them to do X, or if they're required to disclose Y in their SEC filings, or if proposed transaction Z needs to be approved by the board of directors. They may tell us what they're trying to do with a new business model, or in a relationship with another party, and then ask to figure out how to do it.

Here's the basic idea when we do this kind of work.

We look at the relevant actors.

We study the relationships between the actors.

We characterize, from a legal perspective, those relationships.

We identify potential points of intervention in that universe, potential levers we can pull to put the client in a better place.

We create products (documents) that reflect and help implement that advice.

We communicate that advice and transmit our documents to the client.

That's it.

This may not happen all in one fell swoop — the advice may be a product of extended dialogue or otherwise emerge over time or require refinement as the factual situation evolves — but that's the core of it.

This should be a familiar process. As one sees in the first year of law school, much of law seems to be about looking and labeling. We look at an actor or activity, we think about it in view of the facts and the law, and then we put a label on it. And, as we keep looking, we see more, and we add more layers to the analysis

What's different than school is that we are not just looking to analyze but also affect the situation and build products to do just that. Those products help the client get from state A to state B.

Deal Work

Transactions are about moving from current state to future state, too.

The client wants to change its business by way of an event: acquiring another company, selling stock to investors, licensing a technology, spinning-off an internal division into a separate entity. Our job is to figure out how to get it done, and then get it done. A transaction engagement combines advice development with project management.

We have to come up with a transaction structure, which means we need to think about entities, relationships, property flows, tax and other consequences, and contractual and other constraints.

We have to figure out the process, how we get from here to there. That means we need to think about business context, relevant decision-making and regulatory regimes, necessary approvals, contingencies, and timing considerations.

We need to determine what legal products, contracts and otherwise, are required to get the job done. We probably need a bunch of them.

And we need to get all of this accomplished out in the world and on time.

At bottom, deal work involves relationship design and then identifying and coordinating multiple activities involving multiple actors over a stated timeframe. A deal is a big project, and project management is a big part of the job.

Products

In both advisory and transaction engagements, across both corporate and commercial practices, we find ourselves dealing with legal documents. We spend much of our day reading and writing them. They are the products we make for our clients.

Our documents are different than litigation materials. They are business-centered. They tend to reflect (not describe) law, and be directed to readers other than lawyers. They are often jointly written with the other side. They are functional and consequential; people rely on them. They are frequently public and long-lived. They can show up in litigation in varied ways. They can be really long, dense, and difficult. The quality expectations are very high.

There can be a lot going on, and a lot we need to see and capture, in legal documents.

It's useful to think of reading as a fundamental professional activity; we do a lot of reading, and there is real skill involved in reading a document as a lawyer. It's also useful to view documents as products that we build and that do things in the world; there is real craft involved in making them.

Product Range

Our products come in multiple flavors. For simplicity, let's group them in four categories.

Analytical documents help the user assess and understand a problem. They include memos, diagrams, flow charts, tables, timelines, and spreadsheets.

Operative documents do things: transfer assets, define process, set policy, document decisions. They include contracts, corporate bylaws, SEC filings, board minutes, and company policies. They're what we think of when we think of legal documents.

Implementation documents help people understand operative documents and carry out their obligations. They include summaries, checklists, calendars, and cheat sheets. These are designed for use by busy business people.

Communication documents transmit and explain analytical, operating, and implementation documents. They include e-mails, cover memos, and letters. These are often read on smartphones by busy business people.

Awareness of our product range, and a sense of client realities, will help you think about what to make for a client in response to a problem. And it's good to look ahead, to think about and anticipate what documents you may need along the way. If we're thoughtful about it, we can accomplish a lot for our client with our products.

(The variety in our products also suggests two engaging features of corporate practice. First, we get to use our creativity in figuring out and designing the best product for the situation. Second, given that we write both heavy-duty operative documents and concise implementation and communications pieces (the shorter the better), we need considerable facility with language. It's challenging and fun to do both long/technical and crisp/practical.)

Time

Think about how law students are oriented to time periods: semesters, due dates for papers, finals week, on-campus interviews, summer jobs, clerkship application deadlines, bar prep, and so on.

Time-orientation of course is true of corporations as well.

Product development and commercialization are carried out in line with tight product release or "go-to-market" calendars. Financial performance is measured over fiscal periods. SEC filings and lender reports are due within X days after conclusion of a fiscal period.

Background reading materials for directors go out a week before each board meeting.

Transactions are time-oriented. The deal needs to get done by the end of the third quarter. The tender offer must be open for X days. The antitrust authorities require Y days notice before completion of the merger. The proxy statement needs to be mailed Z days before the stockholders' meeting.

Contracts work that way, too. The contact has a term of X years. The product is to be delivered by Y date. If event A doesn't happen by time B, then no payment is due. If party C doesn't object by time Z, then party D is free

to go forward. If borrower F doesn't maintain a specified financial ratio over period G, then F is in default.

This is all obvious. But it's exceptionally important: awareness of organizational, regulatory, transactional, and contractual calendars is central to advice development and deal work.

Big and Little

Corporate practice combines both the big picture and the little picture.

At one level, you're thinking about the business. You study business models. You learn about company, brand, and product strategies. You contemplate corporate structures. You assess organizational risk and operational realities.

At a second level, you focus on legal matters. You study statutes, contracts, and disclosures. You think about the completeness and accuracy of your technical assessment. You work hard on document content.

At a third level, you concentrate on execution on the ground. You make sure every document is in place for the board meeting or transaction closing. You have the phone number for the conference call. You double-check cross-references. You confirm that the numbers add up. You scrub for typos.

Your job, at bottom, is to provide thoughtful advice and products that reflect both big picture considerations and little picture execution.

The ability to operate effectively at multiple levels, to move easily from attention to strategy to attention to detail, is a hallmark of a good corporate lawyer. Your role at each level may change during the course of a project, or from transaction to transaction, or throughout your career as you gain experience in a firm or business. But you'll find that this big/little thing, the ability to work at different levels, is a central aspect of the job.

2 / Visual Thinking and Communication

Making sketches and other visuals is a great thing for us corporate lawyers to do. This chapter, which draws on writing by both practitioners and scholars, explains why.

Sketching? Visuals? Isn't that what architects, engineers, and designers do?

Sketching indeed is what those folks do. But, in many ways, we're like them.

Architects think about buildings and movements of air, light, and people. We think about legal entities and movements of money, goods, data, and intellectual property. Engineers think about mechanical and chemical processes. We create decision-making protocols and transaction plans.

Like architects and engineers, we listen to clients, study the landscape, deal with abstract concepts, draw upon technical knowledge, impose frameworks, develop plans, and build products.

We live in a world of structures, flows, and processes, too.*

* It's interesting that scholars describing the work of transactional lawyers refer to them as "transactions cost engineers" (Gilson) and "enterprise architects" (Dent). Indeed, a 2013 book is called *Law as Engineering: Thinking About What Lawyers Do* (Howarth).

Sketching and Lawyers

"Visual thinking means taking advantage of our innate ability to see — both with our eye and our mind's eye — in order to discover ideas that are otherwise invisible, develop those ideas quickly and intuitively, and then share those ideas with people in a way that they 'get.'"

Dan Roam | *The Back of the Napkin: Selling Ideas and Solving Problems Through Pictures*

Given that, it should not be surprising that corporate lawyers work at the whiteboard. A veteran corporate practitioner (Conboy) observed that "using diagrams is the most common way for an experienced lawyer to train a new lawyer, or to introduce a new lawyer to a deal, a concept, a structure, or a case." He described how diagrams can show a deal structure, or a before-and-after view of a deal, or each step in a series of steps comprising a transaction, or static situations, or relationships among persons and legal entities.

A second deeply experienced corporate lawyer (Weise), in a piece in an American Bar Association publication, identified multiple ways that "lawyers can use drawings to great benefit in their daily work."

Drawing is actually a pretty common practice in the business world. Technology, finance, and other business people, as well as management consultants and investment bankers, routinely draw pictures to illustrate systems designs, networks, data flows, business processes, corporate structures, financing arrangements, and so on. You will go to meetings where the entire conversation centers around a picture on a whiteboard.

So, in view of these parallels with the design professions and the fact that drawings are commonly used in practice (and in business), and given that we don't exactly spend a lot of time in law school talking about visual communication, it makes sense to discuss it in a general way, and then in later chapters offer some specific examples of its value in everyday lawyer activities.

As we'll see, simple sketches and other visuals can be great practical tools for studying a commercial arrangement, working through a set of documents, planning a deal, briefing a partner, or creating a work-product for a client.

Thinking

"[Designers] draw sketches to try out ideas, usually vague and uncertain ones. By examining the externalizations, designers can spot problems they may not have anticipated. More than that, they can see new features and relations among elements they have drawn, ones not intended in the original sketch."

Masaki Suwa and Barbara Tversky | *External Representations Contribute to the Dynamic Construction of Ideas*

There is a lot of writing about sketching and thinking.

There are scholarly books, articles, and symposia in multiple disciplines: cognitive science, psychology, user experience, engineering, architecture, education, design. Topics include "thinking through drawing," "visual thinking," and "graphic thinking." These titles alone suggest why lawyers might want to pay attention here; we're hired to think about things.

There is popular writing, too; the subtitle of a well-known business book is "solving problems and selling ideas with pictures."

Sketching is described as a tool for expressing and trying out ideas, dealing with abstractions, making connections, and preserving ideas and impressions. For lawyers, who deal with abstract concepts all the time, and who routinely impose structure on complex facts, the notion of conveying concepts and structures on paper or screen (through shapes, lines, colors, and spatial relationships) seems quite relevant and interesting.

So is, as one group of scholars (Heiser, Tversky, and Silverman) describes it, the fact that sketches "convert internal memory and mental manipulation to external memory and physical manipulation, relieving limited cognitive resources."

"Relieving limited cognitive resources?" That sounds pretty good for folks who often find themselves working long hours on multiple projects under time pressure.

Discussion Partner

"The process of graphic thinking can be seen as a conversation with ourselves in which we communicate with sketches.… The sketches generated are important because they show how we are thinking about a problem, not just what we think about it."

Paul Laseau | *Graphic Thinking for Architects and Designers*

Sketches, as thinking tools, can help you engage more deeply with a situation.

One writer (Dubovsky) says "drawing is a way of both reflecting on the world and entering in." When you do enter the world (of a business relationship or corporate structure or decision-making process), a visual facilitates productive conversations — with yourself.

Drawing a schematic or a timeline can help bring out what you're thinking and then give you a platform for (internal) discussion about the situation. You look, spot patterns, talk to yourself, make connections, and try out ideas until the assessment or advice comes into better view and that little voice in your head says "I think that works."

Even erasing is helpful in these self-conversations. As one writer (Dee) nicely puts

it, the "ghosts and traces of partial erasure can generate new thoughts and fresh forms." That's really true; that still-visible line you erased ten minutes ago, or that prior version of a mind-map you saved on your phone, may on later encounter prompt a new idea and prove central to your analysis. You have your thinking process right in front of you.

Visuals, in short, provide a ready-made, and always-available, discussion partner.

Collaboration

"The shared sketch … served as a shared focus of attention, ensuring that both partners were considering the same thing. It simplified communication by allowing efficient gestures on the sketch to convey … information instead of cumbersome language. Thus, it allowed for rapid establishment and maintenance of common ground."

Julie Heiser, Barbara Tversky, and Mia Silverman | *Sketches for and from Collaboration*

Sketches facilitate conversations with others, too.

Two scholars (Craft and Cairns), who observed engineers develop information visualization software, noted how sketching "helped to communicate new ideas quickly, to support verbal communication, to confirm understanding, to form a written record for later references, to build complex ideas, and to explain difficult concepts."

Visual representations are "public;" other people can look at, comment on, and easily change them.

Think about standing at a whiteboard with a colleague and how that interaction plays out. You draw, they point, you color, they wave their arms, you cross out, they take the marker and circle something ten times. Then the two of you come back later, look at the board, see something new, revise again, and agree on a plan.

Imagine trying to do that through an e-mail exchange; it's simply not as effective as the two (or five) of you engaging with a picture.

Seeing the Big Picture

"[T]he most salient aspect [of drawings] is their overallness —
the fact that in some sense we see them all at once."

Anthony Dubovsky | *The Euphoria of the Everyday*

Visuals help you see the whole picture.

A sketch can show entities, relationships, movement, and passage of time; it can provide both a broad and a deep view, all at once. Pictures, says one legal scholar (Porter), are very "efficient in conveying information … [with a picture], we approach it from the gestalt perspective, taking it all in at once.…"

Think about how valuable that quality could be when you're trying to understand a transaction structure, or explain it to a client or colleague who asks you for the "30,000-foot view," or develop a multi-month plan for an acquisition.

Litigators like the efficiency of graphics and images, too; as a veteran general counsel (Rosman) notes, "Words may be a lawyer's primary tool, but they're not the only tool.…

A chart can persuasively show factual and legal points, a diagram can explain a case's procedural history, and a photograph can save five pages of your brief."

A little drawing can be great for showing the big picture.

Pictures in the Head

"Drawings can communicate information in ways that words cannot achieve…. Words, sentences and paragraphs are linear — the person reading the words accumulates bits of information one after the other. The reader has to retain each word he has read and then assemble a mental picture bit by bit, one after the other…. The reader constructs his mental picture one word at a time rather than having the opportunity to grasp the 'big picture' all at once…."

Steve Weise | *Get Your Crayons Out*

Visuals can speed up understanding.

People can read pages of text and try to grasp what all is going on, but that can be pretty tough. Imagine a 90-page product commercialization agreement, or hundreds of pages of project finance documents. It's no easy task to follow the action when you're plowing through a pile of paper.

A drawing, which benefits from the power of human visual processing, and which is susceptible to physical manipulation, seems to facilitate faster comprehension. As a legal scholar (Porter) says, "rapid visual cognition of images allows us to understand complex factual scenarios without wading through a ponderous textual explanation."

The everyday expressions we use — "sketch it out for me," "let me get a picture of this in my head" — are telling. Who wants ponderous? Why not, as Weise observed, "skip the words and go straight to the picture?"

Learning Styles and Physicality

"Much of drawing's value derives from its immediacy and its link between what one thinks and one feels…. As drawing is 'pressure sensitive' it dramatizes ideas by making lines more or less intense and emphatic in a manner that reflects the workings of the thought process."

Errol Barron | *Drawing in the Digital Age*

Folks often respond quickly and firmly to questions about their learning styles. Do you describe yourself as a visual learner, one who responds to graphics and images? Did you draw flow charts when you prepared for finals or wrote a paper? Use of sketches, schematics, and other visuals should have obvious appeal to you.

Or, are you a tactile or kinesthetic learner, one who learns best when you're moving or otherwise doing something? And, whatever your learning style, do you retain information better when you take notes by hand? Or when you hold and read a physical book?

Scholars study the physicality of drawing and reading, the connection between hand and mind, and the linkages between touch, movement, and thinking. The act of holding a marker in your hand or moving your finger on a screen, drawing arrows, and erasing and crossing-out, may actually help you get a better grip on a problem.

As one writer (Dubovsky) put it, "the hand-drawn line offers a mode of exploration that goes beyond the mental. The kinesthetic sense enters in — we learn from the physical feel of gesture and movement…. What guides us here — the kinesthetic — is another kind of decision-making, one that develops in the course of action."

In legal work, where we regularly deal with complex situations, we need everything we have to mobilize our knowledge and spark our imaginations. Paying attention to a physical activity that may facilitate cognitive work seems like a pretty sensible move.

You Don't Have to be an Artist

"The sketch is not the end goal. The end goal of the drawing process is what you learn while sketching. So don't worry if you can't sketch. In fact, if you're too good you might just fool yourself into thinking your sketch is a deliverable. It's not. The real value of sketching is that it allows you to explore and refine ideas in a quick, iterative and visual manner with little overhead or learning curve."

Joshua Brewer | *Sketch Sketch Sketch*

Some might question their ability to take advantage of visual techniques because they think they're "not very good at art" or they've "never been able to draw" or they're "not visual types."

Those concerns are irrelevant. For lawyers, sketching is not about artistic skill or personal expression; it's about use of an effective practical technique for getting work done.

Sketches don't have to be fancy. Don't think beautiful drawing or display slide or graphic design software; think scratch paper, whiteboard, tablet, or phone. "Sketches," says one designer (Santa Maria), "are not about being a good artist, they're about being a good thinker."

There is no right way to do it. You can make (or not make) your own rules; boxes for corporations, green lines for money flows, red for risk exposures, purple for relevant statutes, ovals or triangles or arrows or whatever. Diagrams, flow charts, process maps, timelines, doodles, tiny screens or wall-to-wall whiteboards... all are okay.

It just needs to work for you.

Wrapping Up

Making thoughts external? Conveying abstract ideas effectively? Prompting new ideas? Facilitating comment by others? Seeing the big picture? Taking advantage of visual and tactile processing? Portable and available? No rules?

Anything that has such practical utility for creative and collaborative problem-solving ought to be of interest to folks who are paid to think about complicated things, deal with subtle concepts, engage with individuals from other disciplines, come up with workable solutions, and build products.

That would be you.

Sketching can be quite helpful in this line of work, whether you're advising technology entrepreneurs (for whom drawing on a white board is a primary mode of working), presenting a deal structure to a board of directors, or just wading in at the earliest stage of situation assessment. Sketches provide a way to trigger and capture thoughts, engage others, pause, and reinterpret. They help you move from vision to artifact which (like architects and engineers) is what we have to do in this job.

And they work, even in a profession that privileges text over graphic.

You might think of sketch pads (whether paper or touchscreen) as another type of legal pad.

3 / Developing Advice

We lawyers give advice. This chapter suggests a way to think about advice development in a systematic manner.

Advice development occurs across the practice. We may be working with a client on an internal organizational matter, helping draft a communication to a supplier, planning an acquisition, advising a marketer about the use of a tagline or image, negotiating a loan agreement, discussing compliance with a contractual restriction, counseling a board about fiduciary duties, writing a section of an SEC filing, or assessing a potential tort exposure.

In all of these situations we are coming up with advice. The client wants to know what we think, and what we think they should do. We study the situation, do our homework, and come back with ideas and our point of view. Our professional obligation is to deliver competent and independent counsel.

The chapter offers a way of thinking about advice development. As we'll see, the idea here is to come at it by breaking down the situation and then building it back up, in a step-by-step, methodical, layered way.

Actors

Let's start with the actors we encounter in the business world.

Think about what you know about that core actor in corporate practice, the corporation.

It has a perpetual life. It can enter into contracts. It has stockholders, who benefit from limited liability. It is governed by a board of directors, the members of which are elected by the stockholders. It likely is a separate taxpayer from its owners. From a professional responsibility point of view, the corporation itself is your client, not the individual executive who's your contact.

You find that you know a lot about the actor in front of you. And, if it were an LLC or a nonprofit or an employee or a bank or a child, you'd quickly come up with considerable (legally relevant) information about them, too.

Do something that helps you pause and think for just a second about the relevant participants. Maybe drawing a little diagram would help.

By simply reflecting on the nature of the actors, you can quickly start getting a feel for the situation.

Think about what you know about
that core actor in corporate practice,
the corporation.

Internal Dimensions

Look more closely at that corporation. Think about its internal attributes.

On the governance side, it has a formal structure: board, committees, and officers. State law and the entity's organizational documents (articles and bylaws) set out standards and rules, some quite broad in nature (for example, the fiduciary duty of care) and others quite granular (quorum requirements for board meetings). The SEC and stock exchanges impose other rules concerning governance.

As we'll see in chapter 7, there are special governance documents: committee charters, policies, minutes, and so on. Some set out how actions are approved. Others reflect information provided to decision-makers and documentation of those decisions.

The corporation has an internal structure. It might organize itself around geographies,

consumer segments, brands, product lines, or technologies. It may have divisions or units devoted to specific businesses. Most employees are dedicated to core business operations such as product development and marketing, while others focus on finance, human resources, legal, government relations, and other "corporate" functions.

On the operating side, a corporation has endless systems, processes, methodologies, protocols, policies, controls, training regimes, and templates. And of course everywhere there are people: directors, officers, managers, employees, contractors.

These governance and operating features are obviously important from a business point of view; they're essential to planning, management, execution, and reporting.

They're also of considerable interest from a legal perspective. Sometimes they're responsive to specific statutory or contractual requirements. More broadly, they reflect an organization's culture and operating practices — which can be pretty important if there's a tort claim or discrimination allegation or compliance investigation.

From an advice development point of view, these internal attributes can be both hurdles and resources.

They're hurdles in the sense that we may need to jump through an approval hoop or change a practice.

They're resources in the sense that maybe we can use, adjust, or supplement them in an effort to improve the client's position and help the client get to where it wants to be.

Think about the corporation's internal attributes.

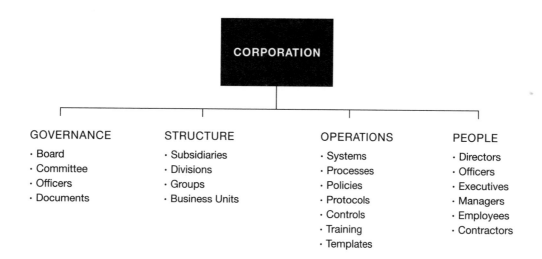

CORPORATION

GOVERNANCE
- Board
- Committee
- Officers
- Documents

STRUCTURE
- Subsidiaries
- Divisions
- Groups
- Business Units

OPERATIONS
- Systems
- Processes
- Policies
- Protocols
- Controls
- Training
- Templates

PEOPLE
- Directors
- Officers
- Executives
- Managers
- Employees
- Contractors

External Dimensions

Think now about the actor's relationships out in the world.

A corporation interacts with stockholders, employees, lenders, suppliers, customers, clients, consumers, competitors, licensees, licensors, alliance partners, auditors, consultants, unions, regulators, the public, NGOs, analysts, media, and so on. Businesses have lots of constituents.

Not just in one state or country, either.

It's obvious when you think about it, but much of what we think about in corporate practice involves those relationships. Our clients engage with constituents in a variety of ways. They may buy services, sell products, raise money, loan money, license intellectual property, advertise to consumers, lobby governments, or communicate to investors. Constituent relationships have multiple dimensions relevant to our work: commercial, financial, reputational, political, and, of course, legal.

As we'll see later, constituency concerns are front-and-center in transaction planning, and the subject of extensive disclosures in SEC filings.

(They also regularly surface in law firm decision-making when firms consider new engagements. Will there be a conflict of interest under the professional responsibility rules if the firm represents, say, a key competitor of an existing client? Or a company that just hired away a group of the client's key employees? And even if there's not a formal conflict, would it just be bad business for the firm?)

A little diagram can help you see constituent relationships that may be relevant to the problem you're studying. It's a great tool for prompting thought about additional dimensions of the problem — and potential ripple effects of proposed solutions. If we do X, what will it mean for constituent A?

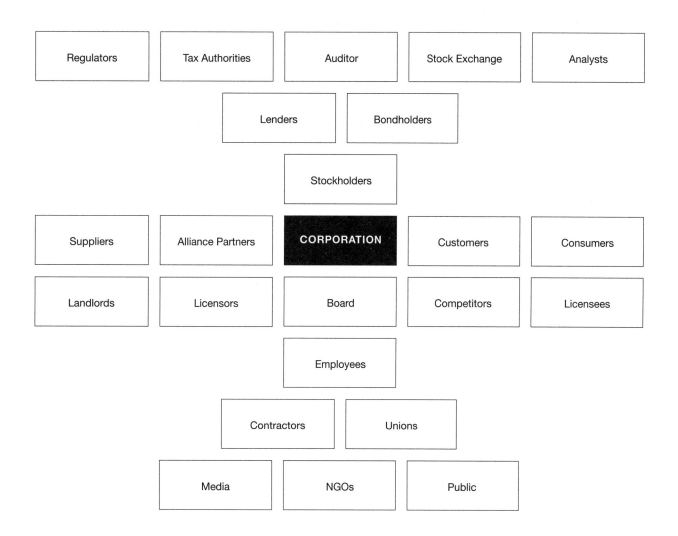

Flows and Characterizations

Let's focus in on the relationships of interest in an advice development setting.

Identify the actors. Identify the flows between the actors. Think physical. What's moving back and forth? Goods? Services? Money? Data? Intellectual property rights?

Then put on your lawyer hat.

How would you characterize those flows from a legal point of view? Sale? License? Guarantee? Dividend (for corporate or tax law purposes)? Restraint on trade? Bribe? What is it? What rules and regulatory regimes are triggered by your characterizations, now and over time?

The L words: looking and labeling. We look at the facts (actors and flows), think about potential legal characterizations, and attach a legal label.

In law school, you learned to study situations and then characterize them. When you took Property, you looked at a piece of land, considered the facts, and then concluded: tenants in common. Or trespass. Or easement. Or covenant running with the land.

Sometimes you found yourself applying multi-factor tests, or stepping back and looking at a series of actions over time that might be seen as an integrated event. And throughout you saw how assessment of an activity can lead to a new understanding of, and (legal) tag for, an actor. The actor is a corporation, but it's also a landlord, or an underwriter of securities, or a franchisor, all subject to special legal regimes.

In all these cases, you stopped, you looked, you labeled.

Same thing here.

What's different, though, is that yet another L word — lever — comes into play. We can start to think about how to improve the client's position. We think about useful interventions, about the levers we can pull, either internally or externally. Maybe we can refine a product offering to avoid an unwanted characterization. Maybe we can change an aspect of a contract, or add a piece of disclosure, or adjust an internal process, to reflect compliance, reduce risk, or improve our ability to defend a position.

We assess these potential approaches, decide on the best ones, and then go create the products (documents) needed to carry out and communicate the selected interventions.

A visual can really be useful here. It can help you identify actors, see flows, step through multi-factor tests, capture multi-event sequences, call out relevant considerations, and spot possible adjustments. A visual can be especially helpful since we're often not just concerned with one doctrinal area; we've got multiple legal (and business) concerns to worry about, and lots of layers to apply.

You might use one color to identify key features of the situation, another for relevant legal authorities and considerations, another for your assessment, another for potential solutions, another for implementation ideas, another for needed documents, and yet another for follow-up questions for the client.

A messy whiteboard, curiously, is often a sign of methodical and systematic analysis. "Dry erase" can be really rich and productive.

Look, label, and find the levers.

1. Identify flows (factual analysis)
2. Characterize flows (legal analysis)
3. Develop interventions (legal advice)
4. Create needed documents (work-product)

Turning Pictures into Words

Maybe you now have a dense and colorful sketch that captures a lot of information and a lot of considered conclusions. That's great.

In some cases, you may be able to clean up the drawing, turn it into a pretty diagram or flow chart, and use that as your deliverable. (Clients tend to love visuals.) In other situations, where a memorandum or letter is more appropriate in view of client context or firm style, you need to get from picture to prose.

A good thing to do when you have the time is to write down a series of numbered, one-sentence assertions. Come up with some basic categories ("Basic Relationship," "Key Legal Considerations," "Accounting Treatment" etc.) and then try to express what you see in simple, punchy sentences, in as logical an order as you can. Don't worry about paragraphs or segues or language; just get the basic facts and considerations stated as crisply as you can.

Such an exercise — which is a sort of hybrid of outlining and writing — pushes you to think logically and write clearly. Telling the story, one step at a time, is hard; this mechanical format forces methodical analysis, structure imposition, and logical organization. Like a sketch, it's a way of mobilizing and memorializing the legal knowledge, diligence, and thoroughness at the core of our professional duty of competence.

It also provides a nifty platform for creating a memo, presentation document, or other traditional work-product. You've already done the hard work.

Write down a series of numbered, one-sentence assertions.

BUSINESS MODEL

1. ABC is a Delaware corporation.

2. ABC provides professional development services to educational institutions and agencies.

3. These services include consulting, training, and provision of digital tools and written materials.

4. ABC's clients include school districts, community colleges, and state agencies.

SERVICE DELIVERY

1. ABC delivers consulting services through in-person meetings, telephone and video-conference meetings, and delivery of written materials.

2. ABC delivers training services through large group meetings, small-group and individual sessions, and online vehicles.

3. ABC delivers written materials in both hard-copy and digital versions.

CONTRACTING PRACTICES

1. ABC when feasible uses its own service agreement form when contracting with clients.

2. In a number of cases (often involving school districts), the client insists on using its own form document.

INTELLECTUAL PROPERTY

1. ABC views its methodology and materials as proprietary in nature and the source of considerable competitive advantage.

2. ABC's contracts provide that ABC makes materials available on a licensed basis, and recite ABC's copyright and other IP rights in the materials.

Example: Introduction

Let's go through an example from commercial practice.

Imagine that ABC is a consulting firm.

ABC offers professional development services to school districts, community colleges, and state agencies. It offers advice, training, and written materials to its clients. It also publishes white papers and the like, and makes them available to the public. ABC views its development approach and reputation as a thought leader as powerful sources of competitive advantage.

ABC has relationships with a variety of companies, nonprofits, academics, and others with whom it works in developing, implementing, and evaluating its methodology and materials.

Intellectual property is at the core of its business. ABC is worried about whether its IP practices, in terms of both development and distribution, are adequate in view of the rapid expansion of its product lines and customer base. It asks you for help and sends you a stack of documents.

Big project here. Where to begin?

You talk with the client, study its website, and take a first look at the docs. You might also think about making use of a whiteboard or touchscreen to help you start getting your hands around constituents, products, delivery vehicles, and other core elements of the business.

Client ABC is a consulting firm.

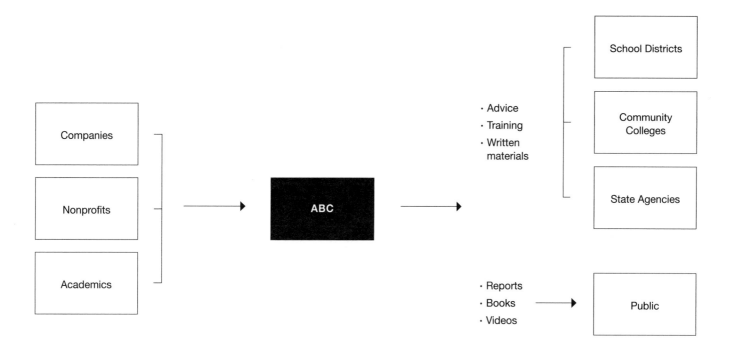

Example: IP Development

You begin at the beginning, by examining IP development. How does ABC create its IP? Where does it get it? You start identifying relevant actors and flows.

You see that ABC develops some IP internally, through its employees.

You see that ABC also obtains IP from third parties. In some cases ABC contracts with firms and individuals for development of specific materials. In other cases ABC collaborates with a third party and engages in true joint development; sometimes those collaborators may use the resulting product in their own businesses.

You note that ABC seems to use more or less the same contract in both situations, and sometimes it has to sign the other party's contract.

You also see that ABC staff draws on academic and other publications in developing materials, and obtains photos and other visuals from a variety of sources.

Start by looking internally, at IP development.

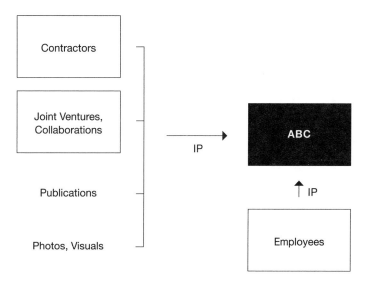

· ABC uses same contract for contractors as well as collaborators.
· ABC sometimes signs other party's contract.

Example: IP Distribution

Then, you look externally, at other actors and flows — this time, outbound dissemination by ABC of its IP. What does it send out? Where does it go? How does it get there?

You see that ABC offers a variety of products and services.

You see that its products include educational materials, evaluation tools, research reports, and books.

You see that its services include formal training sessions, ongoing mentoring support, consulting, and evaluation tool development.

You see that it provides services both in person and remotely through a website, and that it provides some services through third-party contractors.

You see that it transmits materials in both hard-copy and digital versions, and that it's steadily increasing its use of online delivery vehicles.

You note that ABC has a variety of clients, from state agencies to rural school districts.

You observe that ABC sometimes can use its own contracts but that its contract language and website terms aren't particularly well-harmonized.

You see that ABC often must sign the client's form contract, and that sometimes it's operating under massive public agency "request for proposal" documents full of broad-reaching provisions.

You see that ABC regularly receives client, researcher, and public requests for materials. It appears to respond to them largely on an ad hoc basis, and dealing with these requests seems to consume meaningful staff time.

Then, look externally, at IP distribution.

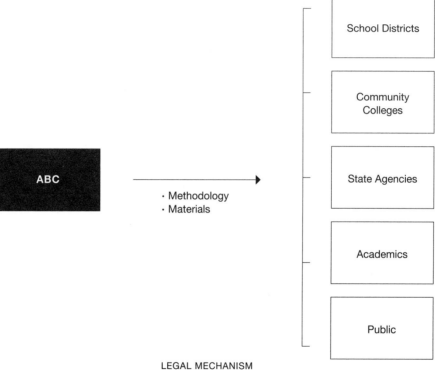

ABC

→ · Methodology
  · Materials

School Districts

Community Colleges

State Agencies

Academics

Public

LEGAL MECHANISM

· Contracts
· Website terms

DELIVERY METHOD

· In person
· Digital delivery
· Hard copy

OTHER OBSERVATIONS

· ABC's contract language and website terms not harmonized.
· ABC often signs client's contract.
· ABC often operates under RFP.
· ABC often responds to requests for materials.

Example: Advice Development

Step back and look at your little diagrams.

You can see a lot. You see in those flows a variety of copyright issues. You see contract issues. You also see potential points of intervention, both internally and externally.

You think about ABC's internal systems. You may want to suggest that the client adopt a general protocol for dealing with IP. How about a "toolkit" or FAQ, posted on the client's intranet, that includes both general guidance and specific responses to recurring situations? It might cover, say, proper use of the little © symbol, incorporation of material from third-party publications, and standard responses to one-off requests. Maybe a short educational video would work well given the client's general approach to delivering employee training.

You think about IP development practices and documents. You may want to suggest that ABC revise its employee confidentiality agreement

to better reflect IP considerations. You might propose that the client accompany the toolkit roll-out with targeted training for employees responsible for IP development and for client interactions.

You might suggest a new template contract, with tighter provisions regarding ABC ownership of IP produced under the contract — as well as alternative provisions for dealing with the subtle copyright and other issues associated with joint development.

And how about a screening tool for use in reviewing contracts and RFPs prepared by third parties? Or a more crisply articulated vendor approval process?

You then think about IP distribution practices and documents. You may want to suggest that ABC revise its client contract template and related digital-delivery website terms to strengthen and harmonize the IP provisions. You

might suggest that it provide clients with simple, business-friendly guidelines about IP use. You might advise them about the use of a Creative Commons license for public materials. You'll likely have a bunch of other good ideas, too.

What's happened here?

You've come up with an assessment, in a step-by-step, easy-to-follow way. You've put a structure on the situation. Your simple analytical sketches helped you activate your knowledge and see a number of places where interventions may be useful. The exercise helped you envision and plan a set of operating and implementation documents reflecting those interventions.

You might also use your sketch as the basis for a communications document, to explain your advice and recommendations to the client; it's likely more effective (and welcomed) than a memo.

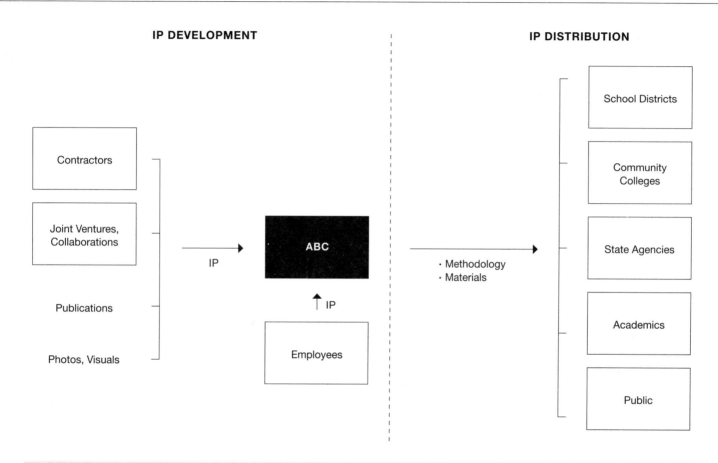

IP DEVELOPMENT

IP DISTRIBUTION

Contractors

Joint Ventures, Collaborations

Publications

Photos, Visuals

IP

ABC

↑ IP

Employees

· Methodology
· Materials

School Districts

Community Colleges

State Agencies

Academics

Public

DOCS

· Revised template contract
· Screening tool for 3rd party contract review

· IP toolkit
· Confidentiality agreement
· Employee training

· New client contract template
· Updated website terms
· Client IP guidelines
· Screening tool for RFP and 3rd party contract review

Stepping Back

Not every advisory situation, of course, has the broad scope of the ABC matter. Oftentimes the question can be quite discrete. A client may call you up and ask "do we have to disclose X?" or "can we include Y in this contract?"

But the basic idea is the same.

We look closely at actors, activities, and events. We characterize under relevant authority. We pause to think about internal and external implications (including opportunities). And we come up with a response.

It's a methodical process of taking apart the situation, one piece at a time, and then building it back up, adding layers as we see more and then designing interventions and creating products that reflect our observations and recommendations.

And, in all these cases, from a practical point of view, it's useful to have a go-to informal technique — whether it's sketching or something else — that helps you get traction, make quick and tangible progress on the problem, and capture what you see.

And Looking Ahead

We'll see this look-label-design-build dynamic not just in straight legal advice settings, where a client wants advice about the law, but also in advisory situations that occur across the practice.

For example, when we're asked by a client if activity X is permissible under a contract, we look at the activity and then characterize it, with the labels coming not from background law but from the conceptual framework established in the contract. When we're asked by a client about the need for a board vote on matter Y, we assess it using the concepts set out in the bylaws as well as the corporation law. And of course litigation (and litigation anticipation) involves looking at a situation and then characterizing it in line with the theory of a claim or defense.

We'll find that the "layering" notion shows up elsewhere, too. Transaction planning, as we'll see in the next chapter, is a giant exercise in adding layers: structure, approvals, timing, documents, and so on. Document work involves consideration of documents on multiple levels: commercial and legal substance, implications, technical execution. Board meeting preparation includes figuring out decision-makers, approval standards, needed information, and meeting mechanics; you build the plan, one layer at a time.

You get the picture: this job draws on your analytical ability, technical knowledge, and imagination. Break it down, and then build it up.

Final Thoughts: Developing Advice

- Look at the relevant actors
- Study the relationship between actors
- Isolate and characterize the flows
- Identify potential interventions (in an actor or the relationship)
- Build the documents

4 / Doing Deals

We lawyers plan and help carry out transactions. This chapter suggests ideas for approaching deal work in a methodical and practical way.

The phrase "doing deals" may conjure up an image of high-stakes negotiations, with intense lawyers at the table all night battling over deal terms and language in big contracts. Counter offers, competing bids, table-pounding, late night calls and e-mails, and the deal finally gets signed up.

Certainly contract negotiations are a big part of deal work, but they're only one part. From a practical (and new lawyer) point of view, transactions can be thought of as big projects.

We do have to get the main contract agreed, but there's likely a lot of homework needed to get to that point, and a lot of planning, coordination, and document prep needed to get past that point to complete the transaction.

New lawyers are deeply involved in those aspects of deal work, and so that's where we'll concentrate our exploration. We'll see how planning and project management are central elements of transactional practice.

Basic Timing

Let's start with timing.

From a when-things-happen point of view, there are two flavors of transactions.

One type involves signing the contract and then completing or "closing" the transaction at a later date. Let's call this a sign-and-close transaction.

Such a contract contains conditions precedent to completion. We sign now, a period of time passes, conditions are satisfied, and then we consummate the deal and transfer value: money is loaned, stock is purchased, assets are transferred, title is conveyed, merger is effective.

A second type involves signing the contract, with value transferring either immediately upon signing or upon a stated date. There are no conditions. Instead, we sign and then go straight to transfer of asset, license of intellectual property, or commencement of relationship. Let's call this type a sign-and-go transaction.

Corporate work, such as M&A and corporate finance, often involves sign-and-close arrangements. The same is true of real estate acquisitions. That's because, as we'll see, those deals often involve obtaining governmental or other third party approvals as a prerequisite to completion. Sometimes that process can

take many months, as in situations involving acquisitions that attract regulatory scrutiny in multiple countries.

Commercial work, whether it's a one-off product sale (for example, an equipment purchase) or an extended relationship (like IP licensing, product distribution, product supply, and real estate lease arrangements), generally involves sign-and-go deals.

We'll focus mostly on the sign-and-close category in this chapter.

This chapter focuses on
sign-and-close transactions.

SIGN-AND-CLOSE

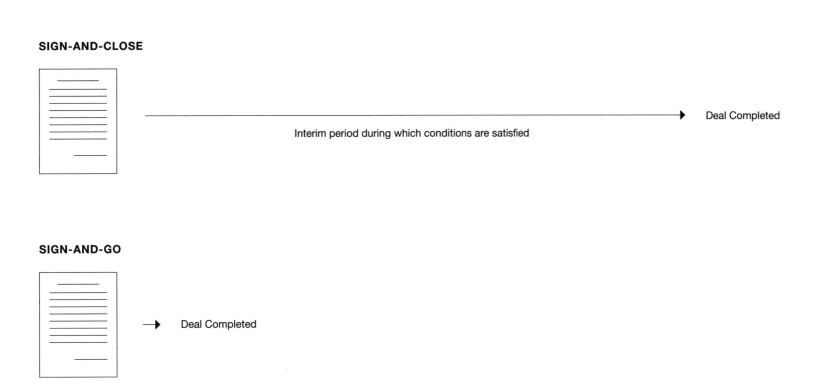

Interim period during which conditions are satisfied → Deal Completed

SIGN-AND-GO

→ Deal Completed

Multiple Transactions

A "transaction" often involves multiple transactions.

For example, asset purchases can involve parallel transfers of goods, real estate, and intellectual property.

Acquisitions where the buyer borrows money it uses to pay the seller involve both a purchase (from the seller) and a financing (from the lender).

Strategic alliances between companies can involve IP licensing, supply arrangements, and equity investments.

Debt restructurings can involve new financings, contract waivers, tender offers, payoffs of existing debt, and releases of security interests.

Mergers and other acquisitions can even involve dispositions. Think about situations where an antitrust regulator requires the buyer to sell certain product lines as a condition to approval of the deal by the regulator. That divestiture activity is a whole separate M&A event going on in the context of the larger transaction.

Internal change can involve multiple transactions, too. Spinning off a division into a separate company includes creating an entity, transferring assets, entering into transition and licensing agreements, and declaring a stock dividend.

In deal settings, you need to study the situation, identify those multiple transactions and parties, and figure out how they fit together. It's like advice development: actors and flows. A little sketch can be helpful in breaking things down.

You'll want to work it through this analysis really carefully. These concerns are foundational in developing the deal plan, including securing the resources you need for each type of transaction that's a part of the festivities.

Identify the various transactions
and figure out how they fit together.

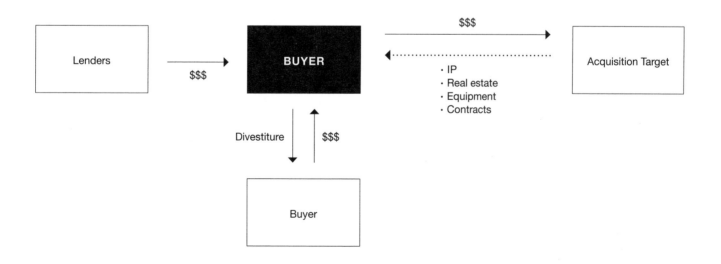

Structure

A related question is deal structure.

Acquisitions, for example, can be executed in a variety of ways: merger, asset purchase, stock purchase. Are the facts such that we best merge two corporations together, buy specific assets relating to the business, or acquire the shares of the entity housing the business?

Debt financings present similar who-and-what questions.

Is it a secured or unsecured loan and, if the former, what's the collateral? Are the borrower's subsidiaries (or owners) on the hook, directly as co-borrowers or indirectly as guarantors? Are any of these persons granting security interests in their assets? And will any of the newly-borrowed funds be applied to pay off existing debt? If so, which debt?

There are a lot of choices in structuring, and a lot of factors drive those choices. Tax planning, liability concerns, licensing and regulatory matters, constraints imposed by existing contracts, and internal organizational features all may be considerations.

There's meaningful homework to be done here. That homework can be intensely technical, with close study of statutes and regs, or deep attention to contract provisions. It can call on heavy-duty application of professional judgment about potential exposures or regulatory objections.

Other times it's really basic: what assets, exactly, are being sold in this deal?

The utility of a visual in this context is obvious — this is where you see partners, investment bankers, and tax experts drawing diagrams. Indeed, it's hard to imagine tax people, who live in a world of exchanges, liquidations, redemptions, reorganizations, and divisions, being able to do much of anything without making use of diagrams.

Transaction structuring involves multiple entities, flows, and considerations. A sketch can capture that complex picture in an efficient way. It helps you follow the action, spot issues, explore refinements and alternatives, and explain the game plan.

Visuals are great for structuring work.

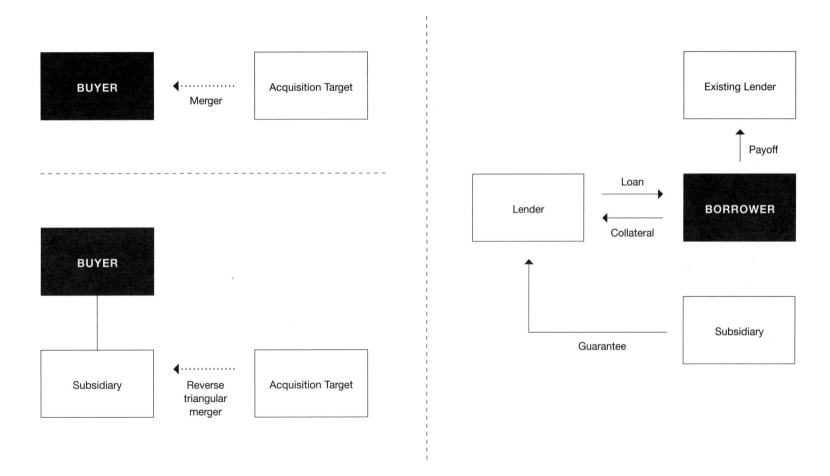

Due Diligence

Folks doing deals together share information.

That makes sense, right? If you're loaning money to someone, you want to know about their finances. If you're licensing your trademark to someone who makes products bearing your name, you want to know about their production, distribution, and marketing capability. If you're buying an entire company, you want to know all sorts of things.

This process of asking questions and finding things out is called "due diligence." New lawyers, especially in M&A and financing settings, are active participants in diligence work.

On the buyer or lender side, associates prepare the request for information from the other side, review the materials produced in response (typically through an online data room), and report on what they find. On the seller or borrower side, they negotiate the scope of the request, help the client gather and organize responsive materials, and assist in responding to questions. (You'll find that in-house lawyers are often deeply involved in this information gathering process.)

Lawyers doing diligence are looking for a number of things. For example, are there any contractual commitments or third party claims that suggest we're not getting what we think we're getting? Or that create exposures we didn't expect? Or contracts that would be breached or that grant the counterparty additional rights if the deal gets done? Or that require us to jump through extra hoops?

The focus is on both the subject matter of the deal and the process for getting it done. What's learned can affect deal terms (including price), risk allocations, and deal planning.

Diligence activity itself presents legal issues.

For example, a company producing information worries about sharing competitively-sensitive information; it requires the recipient to sign a confidentiality agreement limiting use and disclosure. Antitrust regulators get concerned if competitors share information about pricing, customers, and the like. Diligence review of ongoing litigation, potential product liability exposures, and patent validity may involve access to materials subject to attorney-client privilege or attorney work-product protections.

Diligence illustrates how multiple legal concerns can surface even in what appears to be an everyday exercise. These kinds of things can get pretty sticky; you will encounter protocols designed to address them.

When you work on a diligence assignment, you'll want to get clear marching orders. Clients have different takes on (and budgets for) diligence, and your firm may have specific tools for the work. You'll also want to find your own ways (tables, lists, spreadsheets) of keeping track of progress, noting questions, ensuring follow-up, and documenting the work.

Diligence can be dull but it's important to be diligent and organized, in all respects, from beginning to end.

The focus is on both the subject matter of
the deal and the process for getting it done.

BUYER

Acquisition Target

Information

· Are we getting what we think?

· Is this deal permitted under
existing target contracts?

· Does it trigger rights under
any existing target contracts?

· Are there any unexpected
claims or exposures?

· What do they need to do to
get this done?

· Does anything here suggest
a change in deal structure,
plan, or price?

· Do we have to give them all
this information?

· Do we need to worry about
our own confidentiality
obligations to third parties?

· Do we need to put in place
special review protocols?

· Are we providing information
subject to attorney-client
privilege?

· Is there anything in here we
should preview for them?

Constituents

An exceptionally useful exercise in deal planning is to imagine the implications of the transaction for the constituents of the actor: owners, lenders, employees, customers, clients, suppliers, competitors, licensees, landlords, tenants, and so on.

What does this transaction mean for them? What is the business impact, both short-term and long-term? Do we need their help? Do we need to communicate with them? What do we need to do?

For the client, this is a big, big deal: constituent relationship impact will be a central concern.

For the lawyer, it's also a big deal. And it's relevant in all sorts of transactional settings.

A considerable amount of M&A work, for example, involves dealing with constituent impact. Contracts routinely limit assignment and sometimes contain change-in-control provisions that trigger approval, terms adjustment, or even termination rights. The prospect of new ownership, as you can imagine, can be pretty upsetting for employees, licensees, landlords, suppliers, communities, and the rest.

Debt deals require folks to think hard about existing lenders, future lenders, equity holders, affiliates of the borrower. They may all have some claim on borrower assets and cash, and lenders care about competing claims on assets and cash.

Real estate financings find creditors worrying not only about the building owner but also the tenants in the building (and vice versa). They put in place three-way documents with terrifying names like "subordination, non-disturbance, and attornment agreement" to address the implications of the financing, including possible foreclosure, for all involved.

So you may find yourself devoting considerable attention to the topic, on both legal and commercial levels. You need to step through the assessment and, as with proposed interventions in advisory engagements, identify appropriate communications and actions.

Those go into the deal plan.

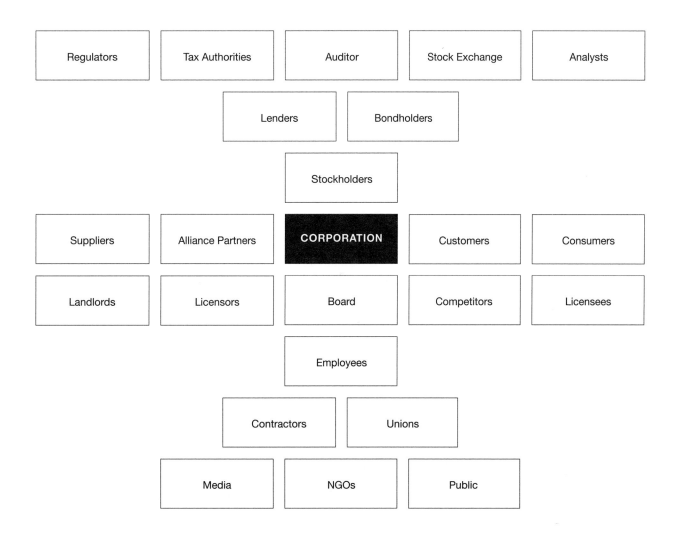

Approvals and Notices

Consideration of diligence concerns and, more broadly, of the internal attributes and external constituents of a transaction party, leads to another wildly important question: who needs to sign off on the deal?

State law, federal law, non-US law, governance documents, and contracts all may impose approval or notice requirements.

In M&A situations, for example, you need board and possibly stockholder approvals under the corporations law.

You may need a clearance from antitrust or other regulatory authorities.

You may need consents from lenders (to deal with loan agreement limitations on fundamental changes in the business or investments), and from landlord and licensors (to deal with anti-assignment and change-of-control provisions in leases and licenses).

This all adds up to a boatload of work.

So you ask: what approvals do we need? What's the process for approval? How long does it take? What information does the approver need? How is the approval documented? Who needs to know about the approval?

And, even if we don't need party X's approval, do we need to give them notice? Or, as a business or reputational matter, should we give them a heads-up, whether we're obligated to or not? If we're dealing with a public company, do we need to worry about disclosing the transaction publicly, or making a filing with the SEC?

Figuring out approvals, notices, and disclosures, and then getting them sequenced, planned, and executed, is a huge part of transactional work. It's a central theme of the script you're writing for the deal.

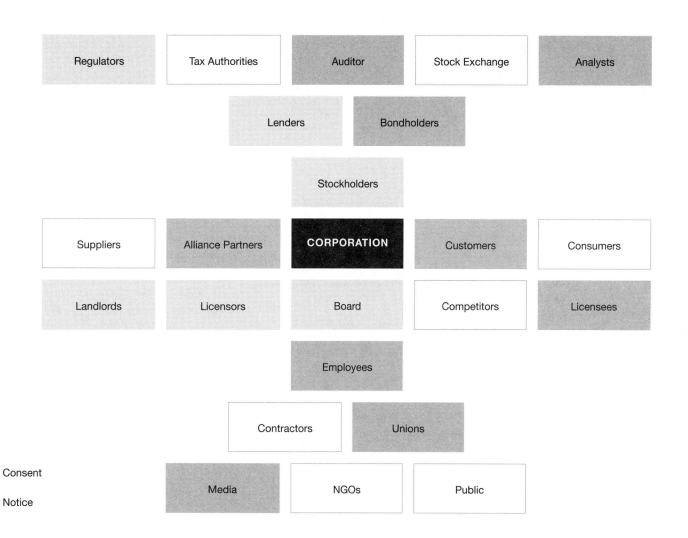

Regulators   Tax Authorities   Auditor   Stock Exchange   Analysts

Lenders   Bondholders

Stockholders

Suppliers   Alliance Partners   **CORPORATION**   Customers   Consumers

Landlords   Licensors   Board   Competitors   Licensees

Employees

Contractors   Unions

Media   NGOs   Public

Consent

Notice

Law

Law shows up in various ways in deal work.

It shapes deal conduct, all those approvals and disclosures, as well as how the parties share information along the way.

It shapes deal structure. You need to design the deal in a way that achieves the desired legal, accounting or tax result (or avoids an unwanted result), or accommodates liability or contractual concerns.

It also of course relates to the legality of the core transaction itself. Does the combination of competitors resulting from this merger create issues under antitrust law? Must the securities offered in this financing be registered under the federal securities laws? Is this technology transfer permitted under national security or export control rules?

It shapes discrete substantive elements of a transaction. Is this provision prohibiting an asset seller from competing with the buyer enforceable under state law? Do the various deal protection features in this acquisition agreement work under Delaware law? Does this provision effectively transfer the intellectual property rights in the deliverable? Will this governing law provision stand up?

This is serious business.

And it's where you see an intersection with advice development. We study the actors and the contemplated flows of value and other activities, and we characterize them from a legal point of view.

We then look for interventions — a refinement in deal structure, a disposition of an asset, a change in contract terms, an added disclosure, a request for an assurance from a regulator — to address the substantive concern.

Same thing: look, label… and find a way to fix the problem.

Look, label, find the levers…
and make sure it's lawful.

1. Identify flows (factual analysis)
2. Characterize flows (legal analysis)
3. Develop interventions (legal advice)
4. Create needed documents (work-product)

Schedule

Figuring out when and how long it takes to get approvals and give notices is a central aspect of deal diligence and planning.

There are plenty of other calendaring considerations as well. The questions always are: what timing constraints do we face? What needs to get done when? What items need to get done before we can do other ones?

These timing factors include core business considerations: fiscal periods, debt maturities, product launch announcements, major marketing events, and so on. No getting around those sorts of things: the client needs to book the deal before the end of the quarter, the company needs to pay back the debt, the market expects the product.

There may be structural considerations such as statutory waiting periods (e.g., providing antitrust authorities with X days' notice before completing an acquisition, or giving stockholders Y days' notice before a meeting), or contracts that require a party to give the counterparty Z days advance notice of a proposed transaction.

The disclosure calendar is important: SEC reporting deadlines or investor or commercial events may affect the plan.

We've seen the need for approvals; we may need to take into account the schedule for board meetings, or regulatory or other third-party approval processes.

The outside world may intrude, with competitive, economic, political, or capital markets events happening during the deal timeframe that might knock us off track.

And we need to think about practical execution considerations such as the internal rhythm of the business, who at the company can know what (and when), management availability, holidays, and even time zones. You may be in California or Illinois but the deal is getting done on New York, London, or Hong Kong time.

There is a lot going on here. A calendar, needless to say, is a wonderful thinking and management tool.

January

February

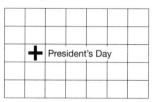

March

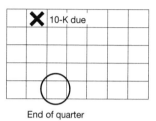

End of quarter

April

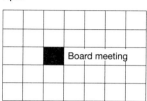

May

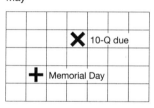

June

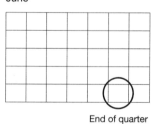

End of quarter

July

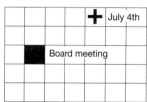

August

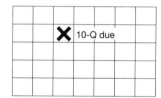

September

End of quarter

October

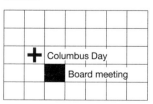

November

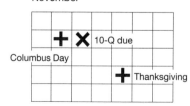

December

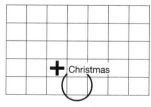

End of quarter

Closings

Let's be optimistic and look ahead to the closing.

Closings, as you recall, are the culmination of sign-and-close deals like acquisitions. They're the big bang where money and assets change hands.

For a new lawyer, closings revolve around documents. Lots of documents. They come in many flavors.

The documents include operative documents that do legal things.

A deed, for example, is needed to convey real estate. An assignment transfers ownership of a trademark. A bill of sale conveys tangible personal property. Other documents may evidence formal consents, approvals, and releases by third parties.

There are documents that provide assurances that everything is in order.

There often is an "officer's certificate," a one-pager in which an officer of one party confirms to the other party that the factual statements in the contract are true and the promises it made are performed. (We'll look at contractual representations and covenants in Chapter 5.)

Another common item is a "secretary's certificate," a document signed by the corporate secretary confirming that the transaction has been duly approved by the board in accordance with the bylaws and other governance documents provided to the other party during the diligence process.

Assurances come from third parties, too.

Sometimes a party is required to produce a formal opinion letter from its law firm regarding corporate approvals, contract enforceability, and so on. (You'll do the back-up work on opinions.)

In some situations, such as securities offerings, the independent auditor for the issuer delivers a "comfort letter" to the purchasers, which addresses various aspects of the audited and unaudited financial information contained in the offering disclosure document.

And oftentimes parties obtain formal confirmations from governmental authorities on corporate good standing, absence of liens, and so on.

The idea with these certificates and letters is to provide comfort to the counterparty that the facts are as represented and the hoops have been jumped through. It's a way to obtain assurances not just from the counterparty in the deal but also from reputable third parties who put their own reputations and credibility on the line. ("Reputation lending," as scholars have noted, is a service provided by lawyers.)

Folks about to make a major commitment understandably want to be confident in the facts and in the process.

(Note: you will see that sellers and borrowers generally have more documents to produce than buyers and lenders. The principal delivery of the latter group is payment, and those providing money are much more concerned about representations and third party assurances than the other way around.)

Finally, there might be some odds and ends like "side agreements" and receipts for payment. Side agreements are just what they sound like; they're a separate agreement covering topics that surface in the course of a deal and don't really fit anyplace else. They might provide additional assurances, or clarify an aspect of the definitive agreement, or include additional promises.

Lots of paper to address lots of moving parts, and all reflective of the high stakes involved. And associates are charged with getting it all pulled together.

(Transactions don't really end at the closing. Thoughtful lawyers know, that while the deal may end for them, it may just be starting for the client. The client has to live with its new partner and with a big document. Operationalizing a contract across an organization, or integrating a new business into an existing business, isn't easy. That's why implementation documents are much appreciated by clients; cheat sheets, road maps, and checklists are really useful to real people.)

Deal Documents

As you stare at that calendar, contemplate deal structure and flows, think about constituent impact, scope out approvals, dream about the closing... such reverie invariably leads one (or at least should lead one) to think about documents.

What all do we need to make to get this done?

We've actually asked ourselves most of those questions already in considering structure, constituents, approvals, and closings.

For example, does the structure require us to create new entities (and thus generate a need for incorporation docs and board materials)?

What contracts do we need? There's likely something called the definitive agreement, which is the principal contract in a transaction. It's the asset purchase, merger, credit, joint venture agreement — the mother ship.

Definitive agreements are often accompanied by ancillary agreements, contracts that relate to aspects of the deal best captured separately. In lending deals, those include security agreements and third party guarantees. In M&A, they may include employment and transition service agreements. (Associates are not ancillary when it comes to ancillary doc prep; they're doing it.)

What assets are moving? Goods? Real estate? IP? Each requires its own special documents.

What internal approvals do we need, for both our client and the counterparty? Do we need our client's board to approve? What information do we need for them? Background memo? Draft resolutions? (More to follow in Chapter 7.)

What external approvals do we need on either side of the deal? Submissions to regulatory agencies? Formal consents from lenders, landlords or other contract parties?

What notices do we need to give to government agencies and third parties? Or employees or unions?

What internal communications do we need? Talking points for management? Announcements to employees? Intranet text? HR packages?

What public disclosures and communications do we need to make? SEC filings? Press releases? Scripts for calls or e-mails to key customers, suppliers, and partners? Do they need to be translated? (Think: constituents.)

Finally (and of central importance to the associate), what certificates and other documents do we need for the closing? And will there be any post-closing filings, with patent and trademark offices, county recorders, and so on?

Paper paper everywhere!

We can take our earlier work and build on it to identify needed documents, the relationships among those documents, the responsibility for preparing them, and the deadlines for getting them done.

Lists are your friends.

YOU TYPICALLY THINK OF

· Definitive agreement
· Ancillary agreements

BUT THERE ARE ALSO

INTERNAL APPROVALS
· Advance materials for board
· Proposed resolutions
· Minutes
· Closing certificates

EXTERNAL APPROVALS
· Regulatory clearances
· Consents from lenders, landlords,
  or other contract parties

NOTICES
· Government agencies
· Communications to customers,
  suppliers, key business partners

PUBLIC DISCLOSURES
· SEC filings
· Press release
· Website copy
· Social media

INTERNAL COMMUNICATIONS
· Management talking points
· Employee announcements
· Intranet text

TARGET EMPLOYEES
· Welcome letter
· Offer package

CLOSING
· Customary closing documents
· Legal opinions
· Post-closing filings

AND ASSET-SPECIFIC DOCS

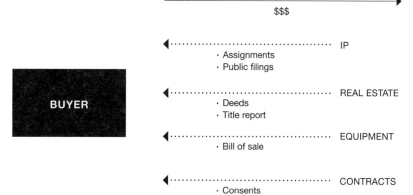

$$$

BUYER

IP
· Assignments
· Public filings

REAL ESTATE
· Deeds
· Title report

EQUIPMENT
· Bill of sale

CONTRACTS
· Consents
· Assignments

Acquisition Target

Pulling it Together

There's a lot to keep track of here.

Timelines and calendars are tough to beat. They are, like sketches, forms of visual communication that help you capture information and see relationships that you may not otherwise see.

Start with the target closing date and then work backward. Add relevant fixed dates (e.g., fiscal period ends, board meetings, bank holidays), and start sketching out needed approvals, assurances, lead times, and public announcements. Start annotating your timeline with the relevant key documents — board materials, regulatory filings, and so on.

You'll end up with another beautifully messy whiteboard. The exercise will help you think it through, and you may find that the process of making that mess will help you internalize, in a way, the mechanics and dependencies in the deal plan.

Perhaps more than any other area, this is where the power of a visual to reveal connections, see "overallness," and facilitate collaboration, really stands out. It enables you to add layers in a visible and tangible way. It's also easy to revisit and revise as the deal takes shape; it's a working tool, and rarely a finished product.

You will find that your calendar will be at the center of the work. Indeed, lawyers and investment bankers regularly prepare "time and responsibility" schedules (a table showing who's doing what by when, often at a granular level) to manage deals, and those documents traditionally have a calendar on the first page.

It's hard to see (and recall) transaction details in your head, especially when you're working on multiple deals and tracking multiple such calendars. And, remember, you need to enlist and engage all sorts of folks to carry out the plan — a calendar establishes common ground.

Start with the target closing date and then work backward.

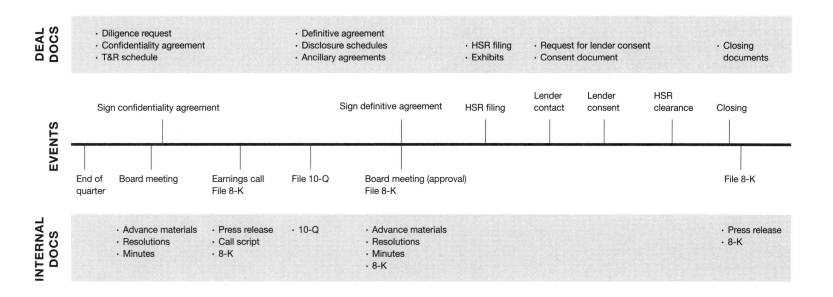

DEAL DOCS
- Diligence request
- Confidentiality agreement
- T&R schedule

- Definitive agreement
- Disclosure schedules
- Ancillary agreements

- HSR filing
- Exhibits

- Request for lender consent
- Consent document

- Closing documents

EVENTS

Sign confidentiality agreement

Sign definitive agreement

HSR filing

Lender contact

Lender consent

HSR clearance

Closing

End of quarter

Board meeting

Earnings call
File 8-K

File 10-Q

Board meeting (approval)
File 8-K

File 8-K

INTERNAL DOCS
- Advance materials
- Resolutions
- Minutes

- Press release
- Call script
- 8-K

- 10-Q

- Advance materials
- Resolutions
- Minutes
- 8-K

- Press release
- 8-K

Project Management

Actually, "engaging folks to carry out the plan" is central to transactional work.

New lawyers are often surprised by the extent to which deal work involves project management. This isn't high jurisprudence; this is running a big project.

Deal work involves constant communication (usually by phone or e-mail), solid organization, and crisp execution. You need a good plan, you have to hit the deadlines on the plan, and you have to make sure others hit their deadlines. (As we'll see in later chapters, project management is a big part of board meeting and SEC filing preparation as well.)

And you need to be mindful of professional responsibility concerns; you shouldn't be communicating with the principals on the other side unless you have consent from their lawyer, and you need to do the right thing on everyday stuff like providing reasonable lead times and announcing if other folks are in the room on a conference call.

(If you need documents and signatures from your client, be sure to give them the heads-up and plenty of time. Last minute scrambles are not welcomed.)

It's your job to get the deal closed, and to do it in the right way.

Organization, reliability, consideration for others, trustworthiness, tenacity, attention to detail, patience (and occasional impatience), good attitude, and a willingness to help out, are valuable personal qualities to bring to this sort of thing. There's a fair amount of just grinding it out, and there are plenty of opportunities to help others grind it out.

That acknowledged, there can be real intellectual and professional satisfaction in deal work. It's fun to solve what often is a pretty complicated puzzle, to lead a group under pressure, and to get the client to where it wants to go.

Organization and self-discipline are also helpful on other levels. If you do your planning, if you keep things organized, if you get your pieces done on time (or earlier)… you'll not only make life easier for your clients and colleagues but you'll have a better chance of getting home to your family or over to the gym or out for a bike ride. Which are very good things.

Building Things

Recall the earlier comparison of designers and engineers to lawyers.

Construction is a great way to think about transaction planning.

We're architects, because we listen to client ideas and goals, envision structure, imagine impacts on the neighborhood, and create imaginative plans to achieve the client's vision (and meet code).

We're general contractors, because we study the blueprint, identify and coordinate needed materials and services, and manage the project. There are multiple moving parts, and it's our responsibility to coordinate the work and see that it gets done.

And, we're carpenters, because we execute skilled technical work in assessing legal complexities and, especially, creating deal documents with our hands.

At the end of the project, we get to visit the site and see a new business or a new balance sheet or a new product line that we helped to design and build.

Final Thoughts: Doing Deals

- Identify deal flows

- Determine deal structure

- Study impact on constituents

- Identify needed approvals and communications

- Make list of documents

- Work backward from the closing

- Develop timeline

- Manage the project

5 / Thinking about our Products

Documents are the products we make for our clients. This chapter offers some observations about their features and functioning.

Legal documents — our products — are quite different from the litigation materials encountered in law school.

For us, the context is generally collaborative and business-oriented in nature. It often involves no opposing party at all; instead, it's just us and the client.

Our documents are grounded in business. They tend to reflect, not describe or discuss, law. They set out plans for relationships, define decision-making processes, and communicate to the market.

Unlike litigators, we generally write for audiences other than lawyers. Our readers include not only clients but also all those corporate constituents: investors, lenders, customers, suppliers, employees, auditors, regulators, and media. Most of our work doesn't have our name on it. Instead, it's the client's document, and has the client's name on it.

People use our documents in their work, and they rely on them.

Let's take a closer look at these things we make for our clients.

Mostly Business

Legal documents are mostly business documents.

They're full of plans, processes, facts, and numbers.

Documents set out roadmaps for relationships.

They specify how one party can employ another's property (lease, loan, license), or reflect the path by which a product is brought to market (commercialization), or concern a particular business function (outsourcing), or set out a deal plan (time-and-responsibility schedule). They describe how services are delivered, how money moves, how transactions are executed.

Documents are often about process.

Research and development agreements include procedures for information exchange, joint decision-making, and cost-sharing. Licenses define product and marketing approval regimes. Acquisition and financing documents set out the mechanics of asset transfers and funds flows.

Contracts among stockholders detail voting agreements and information access rights.

Not much overt law here; mostly process.

And it's not just contracts.

Bylaws provide a framework for how boards make decisions. Equity compensation plans specify procedures for exercise of stock options. Employee benefit plans include eligibility, participation, and grievance rules.

When you draft a document, especially a commercial contract, or you give advice about a proposed new business model, you often find yourself asking a client: "so how does this work?" You have to capture (and often create), processes and mechanics. Which means that logical, step-by-step thinking is the order of the day.

Documents can contain lots of facts.

As we'll see, contracts may contain lengthy factual statements by one or both parties.

Materials for boards of directors are full of strategy, operating, and financial data. SEC filings contain page after page of information about a company's financial results, products, customers, competitors, management, and so on.

Documents often embody marketplace practices and standards. A client or other party in a negotiation may ask "what's market for that?", a question that reflects the influence of commercial practice and market conditions on contract provisions.

Documents not only reflect but also speak to the market. Disclosure documents, privacy policies, and other materials communicate to constituents, help set expectations, and shape company and brand perceptions.

Legal document work is business work. This may be one of the many reasons clients say the most important thing is for my lawyer to understand my business.

Functionality

Documents are highly functional. They can do a lot of work.

Think, for example, about all the things that contracts can do.

As you saw in your Contracts class, contracts can set out business terms — price, quantity, delivery time — and they can provide for future contingencies.

Contracts can do more. They can transmit information, describe ongoing interactions, help achieve a desired legal status or accounting or tax result, help reflect compliance with (or contract around) background law, help demonstrate diligence, and help avoid conflicts with other contracts.

And, if things get dicey, contracts can also help avoid derivative liability arising from the conduct of the other party, provide a transition mechanic at the end of a relationship, provide a remedy if there's a breach, and provide litigation tools if things go sideways.

These are pretty functional devices.

Corporate governance documents can do a lot of work, too.

Board minutes, as we'll see, can reflect not only formal board approval of item X but also document the information base for the decision, the deliberations, any needed factual findings, and compliance with technical approval requirements. You can use board resolutions to delegate authority to board committees or officers to take future action in respect of item X should the need arise.

Analytical, implementation, and communication documents can do a lot of work as well. Consider, for example, how use of implementation documents might help a client not only reduce the risk of a problem (by guiding employees) but also demonstrate its reasonable care if there is a problem.

The task (and creativity) in making these things is in thinking about how much we can accomplish for the client, now and in the future. What work can we do? What's the best vehicle? And how do we best leverage this vehicle to benefit our client?

Remember, there are few bounds on what we can make for a client. Our products come in tremendous variety. Part of the fun is figuring out what's best in the situation and having the facility with words to move easily from giant technical contract to one-page cheat sheet, all with the goal of doing as much as we can for the client.

Consequences

Documents have consequences. The lawyers may move on, but the client has to live with it.

Contracts may require organizations to understand and internalize complex rules.

A contract may require a party to monitor, compute, and report on a variety of quantitative measures, and to not exceed (or fall short) of specified levels. It may set out multiple events that require Party A to notify or get the approval of Party B within a specified period. Or it may provide for multiple trigger events that demand quick and serious decision-making.

Parties can face meaningful strategic and operating challenges when subject to contractual rules, and practical challenges in recognizing and acting on contract-relevant situations. This is not easy to do across a big organization. It's one reason implementation documents are so useful.

A document can create big trouble under another document.

The terms of one agreement may violate the terms of another contract, or a default under one agreement may result in a default under one or more other agreements. That's a nasty thing called a "cross-default." (The reality of conflicting documents is a good reason to be diligent when doing diligence, and is why contracts, legal opinions, and officers' certificates often address this topic.)

Contracts can affect tax and accounting results.

For example, contract terms are a key factor under the accounting rules in determining whether a company can recognize revenue from a sale transaction, which is about as fundamental an accounting assertion as there is. Contracts and employee plans are often described in the notes to the financial statements; you may find yourself writing those disclosures.

Public companies, as we'll see in chapter 9, are obligated to disclose information about key contracts and even file them with the SEC, for all the world to see.

Financial disclosures affect market perception and expectations, set precedents that bound future external reporting, and may be the subject of securities fraud claims.

Compliance program policies and employee training materials may reduce the risk of prosecution or provide a mitigating factor in a corporate criminal case.

And, at a very human level, people rely on advance directives to guide their treatment as they near death, and on wills and trust instruments to dispose of their assets as they direct after they die.

Documents can have broad footprints. You need to be on your toes.

Visibility

Legal documents aren't just hiding in filing cabinets, sitting on hard drives, or residing somewhere in the cloud. They're often quite visible.

SEC filings by definition are public, and instantly available upon filing.

Public company governance materials and privacy policies are posted on the company website.

Articles of incorporation and UCC financing statements are available through the state government.

Real property ownership, easement, and security documents are retrievable at the county registrar of deeds (recall from Property the importance of "notice").

Product performance warranties are on the package and safety warnings are on the product.

Even internal documents are visible.

Board materials and minutes, as we'll see, are reviewed in the ordinary course by auditors, examined in due diligence reviews by potential acquirers and lenders, provided to regulators, and discoverable in fiduciary duty and other litigation. That can sometimes also be the case even with respect to our own e-mails, memos, drafts, and other communications to the client.

Think of all those corporate constituents out there; they are potential readers of your documents.

Lawyer work is routinely on display, which can be rather sobering. And it's really, really important to bear in mind that documents are read in different contexts at different times by different persons with different agendas. That recognition and spur to thought is a central aspect of this sort of work.

We have to think about all those readers; as with constituency analysis in deal planning, it's a corporate manifestation of the familiar lawyer stance of considering situations from others' point of view, and adding additional layers to the analysis.

Long Life

Documents can be long-lived. A good portion of our writing is ephemeral in nature (for example, receipts and certificates delivered at a closing) but many documents can have a long and consequential life.

Think about corporations: entity creation documents result in legal persons with perpetual life.

Think about real estate; easements on land can last forever, and a commercial lease may have options extending far out in time.

Think about debt: bonds may not be due for years, and residential mortgages are effective for decades.

Think about joint ventures and licenses: they may contain exclusivity, field of use, or non-compete provisions extending over multiple years that may create complexities (and heartburn) as businesses and markets evolve.

Think about disclosures: SEC filings for single periods nonetheless provide the foundation for quarter after quarter of later reporting.

Document longevity and visibility suggest the importance of competence, imagination, diligence, methodical analysis, precision, and seriousness.

You're often building for the long term, and on a public street.

It's Group Work

Documents routinely are the products of collaborative work.

Contracts are prepared by at least two parties.

Stock offerings involve group drafting by roomfuls of businesspersons, accountants, investment bankers, and lawyers.

Alliance and joint venture agreements, SEC filings, corporate policies, and employee communications are the products of multiple functional units within an organization.

Documents are subject to critical reading, testing, and comment by multiple readers from diverse disciplines at different times. You will often find yourself charged with "keeping the master," which means you're responsible for tracking and dealing with all the input.

Your readers are vocal, about everything, from business point to comma placement. They provide comments in a variety of forms: orally in meetings or calls, voicemail messages, e-mails, track changes versions, inserts, handwritten mark-ups.

The abilities to anticipate reactions, incorporate comments received in varied forms (and resolve conflicting comments), deal with both the dreaded "conceptual" comment and the nit-picks, persuade others about (and be flexible concerning) language choices, and communicate in an efficient and practical way, are basic competencies of the trade. So is not taking any of this personally.

Document work is often a multi-participant, multi-draft process requiring stamina, concentration, collaboration, patience, good cheer, and occasionally a thick skin.

There's Some Law, Too

Law surfaces in various ways in documents. Unlike our litigator friends, we don't write much about law (not a lot of "In *Smith vs. Jones*, the court held..." phrases in our world), but it's still in our documents.

Let's start with something obvious. Some documents break the law, such as contracts in "restraint of trade" under the Sherman Act.

There of course are big bodies of law about the meaning, interpretation, and effectiveness of legal documents: think contract law, or trusts and estates.

Law may concern the existence, content, and form of documents.

Statutes compel companies to create specified documents and dictate the subject-matter and form of those documents. As we'll see, that sums up the disclosure regime under the federal securities laws, and it describes incorporation requirements under state corporation laws.

Statutes both require and forbid the inclusion of certain terms in contracts, and impose

standards for how they're written (even the typeface size). This is seen in consumer protection and other areas, including our professional responsibility rules.

Judicial opinions influence document content and language. This one surfaces all the time; for example, liability limitation and boilerplate provisions in contracts are routinely litigated, and decisions by state courts (especially in Delaware) interpreting corporation law influence provisions in M&A agreements and corporate bylaws.

Law may require use of specific documents to achieve desired results; under the Uniform Commercial Code, for example, a lender may need a security agreement and financing statement to create and perfect a security interest in personal property.

Law shapes entity structure and governance; documents such as articles of incorporation, bylaws, and LLC operating agreements reflect underlying corporate law requirements.

Contracts create legal obligations, but law is seen in contracts in ways going beyond contract law. For example, an acquisition agreement may touch upon multiple doctrinal areas, from environmental law to employee benefits. That's one reason M&A deal teams are so big.

Compliance with law can be the subject of documents. Acquisition and financing agreements include factual statements and promises about compliance with legal requirements, and transacting parties may demand assurances about contract enforceability and compliance with relevant legal regimes.

Finally, as we'll see in later chapters, provisions in contracts and other documents can directly affect litigation options and outcomes.

Law is there, but mostly it's underneath, not front and center, in legal documents. Part of the art is learning to see the law, to see how law manifests itself in the content, form, and consequence of the document, and to deal with it thoroughly and thoughtfully.

Law surfaces in various ways in, and operates mostly underneath, legal documents.

- · Document may break the law
- · There may be a big body of law about meaning and effect of document
- · Law may require creation of document
- · Law may require use of certain document to achieve specific legal result

- · Law may dictate content and form of document
- · Law may forbid inclusion of specified content
- · Law may require inclusion of specified content
- · Some content may be subject of extensive caselaw

- · Document may touch on multiple doctrinal areas
- · Document may shape litigation options and potential remedies
- · Documents may be admissible and have different forms of evidentiary value

They're Hard

Working with documents can demand considerable intellectual and emotional effort.

Documents may call for great breadth in content knowledge.

Comprehension of some commercial agreements, for example, requires knowledge of technical and industry terminology and concepts, regulatory processes in multiple jurisdictions, marketing laws and business practices in the industry, accounting principles, and patent, trade secret, trademark, and commercial law principles.

Documents may require pretty serious analytical aptitude.

Giving advice about the feasibility of a transaction under a set of financing instruments, say, requires considerable facility with abstract and interrelated concepts. A transaction plan requires identification, analysis, and sequencing of multiple organizational, operating, approval, disclosure, notice, and other factors. Lots to keep in mind here.

Documents may require heavy-duty technical review and writing.

Financing, product commercialization, and other agreements may have 30 or 40 pages of defined terms involving accounting, scientific, technical, privacy, and other matters. Individual defined terms are then incorporated in other defined terms which are used in provisions that cross-reference other provisions which include exceptions and provisos and require computations for specified time periods.

This is a reality that tests not only abstract reasoning abilities but also the ability to write with precision and care.

Document can require a lot of on-the-ground homework.

Formal legal opinions demand intensive behind-the-scenes work; there is a substantial literature regarding the meaning of, and work required to deliver, individual sentences in legal opinions. Even one-page documents can require substantial diligence; as we'll see, corporate officer certifications regarding SEC filings involve broad statements about disclosure accuracy, internal processes, and legal compliance. These executives will be counting on you when they make those confirmations.

It goes without saying that legal documents can be long and boring.

The lawyer needs to read all the way through, which gets even harder when documents go through multiple drafts. A critical part of a document may be a business-focused exhibit way in the back, or a boilerplate provision that in context has a substantive effect on the deal or later litigation.

Finally, legal documents are highly polished (and often terribly expensive) pieces of writing.

Expectations for written work are exceedingly high. Sloppy work gets exposed, in the drafting process, in diligence, at a closing, or, worse, by the client or during a dispute or lawsuit. There is a premium on accuracy, organization, internal consistency, precision in language, and technical execution.

You cannot give enough attention to attention to detail.

It's no surprise that coffee shops near law firms do a nice business. And it's no surprise that the term "diligence" appears in both case law and professional responsibility rules regarding lawyer duties of care and competence. You really have to bear down on these things.

Legal documents can be long and boring.

exceed $15,000,000 in the aggregate at any time outstanding; provided, however, that for all purposes under this Section 7.14 all direct and indirect references to "Limited Guarantors" shall exclude foreign branches of Limited Guarantors; provided further, that (i) the requirements of this Section 7.14 (other than the requirements of Section 7.14(d)) shall not apply (A) during any Minimum Excess Availability Period (I) occurring during the period beginning on the Amendment Date and ending on the Trademark Subfacility Payoff Date (so long as (x) after giving effect to any proposed Investment, Availability would not be less than $100,000,000 with respect to intercompany transactions or $125,000,000 with respect to third party transactions and (y) immediately before and after giving effect to any proposed Investment, no Default or Event of Default has occurred and is continuing) or (II) occurring during the period beginning on the date after the Trademark Subfacility Payoff Date (so long as (x) after giving effect to any proposed Investment, Availability would not be less than $25,000,000 and (y)immediately before and after giving effect to any proposed Investment, no Default or Event of Default has occurred and is continuing), or (B) to any Investments made or held with the proceeds of the issuance of Equity Interests of Borrower or any Foreign Subsidiary, (ii) no Default or Event of Default shall be deemed to have occurred following any Minimum Excess Availability Period based solely on any Investments made during any Minimum Excess Availability Period and any such Investments shall not be taken into account when applying the dollar limitations set forth in this Section 7.14, and (iii) notwithstanding the foregoing, the requirements of Section 7.14(n) (other than Section 7.14(n)(ii)(A)(1)) shall continue to apply during any Minimum Excess Availability Period to Consolidated Investments (other than Consolidated Investments, the purchase price of which does not exceed, in the aggregate, $15,000,000

Scary but Sensible

Business, process, consequences, visibility, comments, law, details, boredom… we need some good news here.

We've got it.

Let's start by observing that legal documents may be long, dense, and downright daunting, but the concerns reflected in the documents are often pretty commonsensical.

You can get traction on understanding a document by simply imagining what the parties would be concerned about in the circumstances.

What would you worry about if, say, you were loaning money to somebody?

You'd obviously need to figure out the basic business terms: principal amount, interest rate, due date, frequency of payments.

You'd probably worry about the borrower's behavior (you'd tell them don't make bad decisions, don't make big changes without asking me) and financial performance (be sure to generate plenty of cash), about others who may get cash from the borrower or have claims on its assets (other lenders, future lenders, equity holders, affiliates… so pay me first), and about what you can do if there's a problem (pay me now).

Cash in, cash out, asset location, competing claims, a hammer. That's about it, right?

As it turns out, that's pretty much what you'll find in a loan agreement.

Those concerns will be captured in the form of business terms, factual statements and promises by the borrower, and a set of events which, if they happen, enable you to drop that hammer.

You'll see the same sort of thing in commercial agreements. Office leases, for example, are full of provisions addressing space, term, renewals, rent, use, utilities, parking, repairs, alterations, subleasing, damage, and so on.

Governance materials are pretty straightforward, too. Who decides? How do they get chosen? How do we call a meeting? How many votes do we need?

Nothing very magical here. The question is, what practical things do you need to cover, and what are you worried about?

Thinking about a contract or other legal document in this way, and integrating those common sense understandings with your substantive legal knowledge, can help you deal with what otherwise can be intimidating materials. (It also gives you good ideas for how to explain the document to your client.)

Use your common sense and imagine what the parties would be concerned about.

- How big is the loan?
- What's the interest rate?
- When must they pay it back?
- When are interest payments due?

- Do they have authority to do this deal?
- Is this consistent with their other obligations?
- Do they own their assets free and clear?
- Do they owe other people money?
- Are their financials good? Have they paid their taxes?
- Are they in compliance with law?
- Are they getting sued by anybody?

- What can they do with the money?
- Can they still borrow money from others?
- Can they pledge their assets to someone else?
- Can they sell their assets?
- Can they change their business or buy another company?
- Will they send financial reports and updates about their business?
- Do they have to maintain minimum financial performance levels?
- Will they keep their assets protected and pay their taxes?

- What happens if they don't pay on time?
- What happens if they break their other promises?
- What happens if they haven't told the truth about their business?
- What happens if something really bad happens in their business?

Standard Components

The second piece of good news is that core documents use a standard set of parts.

Contracts, for example, have common components. Some are straightforward — for example, the introductory section setting out the parties' name and entity type — but others allow you to do all sorts of things.

Recitals, for example, let you frame deal background and intent. You can tell the story of the deal.

Representations let you require the other party to make wide-ranging factual statements. You can get them on the record.

Covenants enable you to set out rules about their behavior. They're just promises.

Conditions let you give your client routes out of a deal through establishing prerequisites to performance. If X doesn't happen, the client doesn't have to go forward with the deal.

Indemnification enables you to protect your client from claims based on the other party's performance. Something bad happens, your client gets sued or damaged, and the other party is on the hook to take care of it.

Liability provisions let you bound exposures and shape remedial options. You can try to limit the downside (and to give your client a hammer).

Termination provisions let you create ways for your client to get out of a deal or exit an ongoing relationship because of problems in performance, events affecting the other party, or occurrence of external events. Something bad happens… your client can move on.

Boilerplate lets you give a court instructions about how to interpret the contract. Waivers must be in writing, and New York law governs.

Schedules and exhibits let you set out facts, disclose exceptions to the representations, provide sample calculations, and reflect agreement on the form of ancillary and closing documents. They're useful vehicles for capturing all kinds of things.

You can do a whole lot more with these basic contract components, too. They are handy little critters.

And they become familiar pretty quickly.

You see them over and over. You'll see both patterns in their use and coverage (which reflects, in part, the common sense of deal terms and the existence of marketplace standards) and opportunities to deploy them in creative ways.

For a lawyer, the parade of reps, covenants, and conditions becomes second nature, as do the time-and-responsibility schedules of deal work, the certificates found at a transaction closing, and the governance and disclosure materials we'll touch upon later in the book.

Like any other trade, you just need a little time to learn your way around the product and the parts room.

CLASSIC CONTRACT COMPONENTS

COMPONENT	DESCRIPTION	DETAILS
Introduction	Gives the basics	· Name of agreement · Date of agreement · Parties · Nature of parties
Recitals	Tells the story of the deal	· Background · History · Objectives
Business terms	Describe the deal	· Asset · Price · Quantity · Payment · Time · Rights
Reps	Are about facts	· Reps are statements of facts · Warranties are promises that statements are true · Reps convey information and induce reliance
Covenants	Are promises about conduct	· Promise to do something (affirmative) · Promise not to do something (negative)
Conditions	Are prerequisites for performance	· If conditions not satisfied, then party not obligated to go forward

COMPONENT	DESCRIPTION	DETAILS
Indemnity	Is about protection	· Promise by which one protects another from a legal consequence of the conduct of a party or other person
Liability and remedies	Shapes litigation outcomes	· Limit recoverable damages · Limit (or provide) remedies
Termination	Is about the end game	· Sets out circumstances when one party can terminate contract or when contract terminates automatically · May also provide for consequences
Boilerplate	Is the (important) legal stuff in the back	· Contract interpretation including entire agreement, waiver, and severability · Amendment · Dispute resolution including tribunal and governing law
Signature blocks	Are about confirming agreement	· Identifies name of signatory · Identifies capacity of signatory · Satisfies statute of frauds
Schedules and exhibits	Do lots of things	· Set out business information · Respond to reps (exceptions, required disclosures) · Contain sample computations · Provide forms of ancillary and closing documents

Standard Organization and Conventions

Yet another good thing is that legal documents often have not only standard components but also characteristic organizational schemes and conventions.

That big credit agreement, for example, will no doubt have sections devoted to business terms, representations, conditions, covenants, and events of default.

Some of the covenants (known as "affirmative" covenants) require specified conduct by the borrower. Others ("negative" covenants) limit conduct; they typically contain flat bars on certain behaviors followed by a series of exceptions. Still others ("financial" covenants) require the borrower to meet financial performance levels and ratios.

The agreement likely will have lots of defined terms, and many of the provisions (especially the covenants) will refer to each other.

An acquisition agreement will have business terms up front and then sections devoted to

reps and warranties, covenants, conditions, termination, and indemnification, with disclosure schedules and exhibits attached.

In both financing and acquisition agreements, you'll see linkages between the sections: the conditions won't be satisfied unless the reps are true and the covenants are performed. This linkage makes good sense; if someone lied to you or didn't do what they promised to do, wouldn't you want the ability to get out of the deal?

Because of their variety, commercial contracts have more varied organizational schemes, but you can see a general pattern. They tend to follow the life of the relationship, the road from occupancy to eviction, from idea to product to problem.

A trademark license, for example, will begin with the common sense business terms of the license: licensed mark, use, term, territory, compensation. That's followed by provisions

relating to ownership and protection of the trademark, the path of the licensed product to market (development, sourcing, marketing, and distribution), liability allocations in the event of infringement or injury, termination, and dispute resolution.

Think of it as, well, dating to divorce, happy to sad...

In both corporate and commercial documents, you'll see business terms up front, and typically an ascending attention to "legal" stuff (indemnification, termination, dispute resolution) as you move along. Price, term, and quantity on page 1, the boilerplate on pages 64–66.

Documents have characteristic organizational schemes.

SIGN-AND-CLOSE

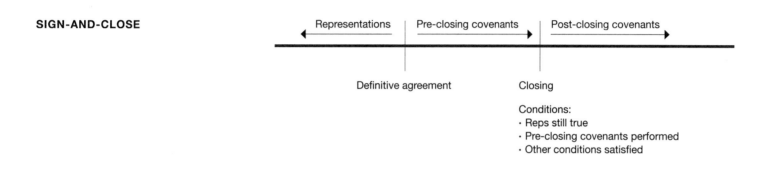

CONTRACTS GENERALLY

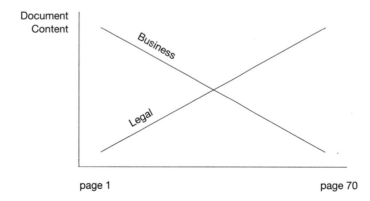

We Can Do This

Documents are the products we review and make for clients.

They're full of business. They manifest underlying legal rules and external influences. They do a lot of work. They are visible and have consequences in the world. They are read by all sorts of readers in all sorts of contexts. They are highly polished. They are written by groups. They can be really long and difficult.

The good news is that common sense gets you a long way in understanding them. As does learning the characteristic components, organizational schemes, and conventions of the materials you regularly encounter in your practice. We'll see in the next chapter a variety of practical ways for getting a grip on even the biggest and most daunting of these things.

And, if it makes you feel better about our products, do know that corporate lawyers almost never touch the Bluebook after law school.

Final Thoughts: Thinking about our Products

- Learn the business

- Think about the common sense underlying the document

- Think about the work being done by the document

- Think about the law under the document

- Think about potential readers

- Know characteristic components, organizational schemes, and conventions

6 / Working with our Products

This chapter offers some ideas about ways to deal with existing documents and create new ones.

Let's continue our discussion of documents by noting something obvious but hugely important.

If you think about it, reading is a core lawyer activity.

We actually spend most of the day reading. We read client materials, statutes, regulations, diligence materials, SEC filings, drafts received from the other side of the deal, our colleagues' work-products, our own drafts, e-mails, website copy, and all kinds of other things.

The products of the trade are documents, and we engage with them through reading.

Much of what we think of as legal work involves reading. Oftentimes, it literally *is* the work; lawyers are regularly retained to read documents. It's pretty wild, actually, that clients send materials to us, instruct us to read them, take action based on what we have to say about them, and then pay us.

We've seen that there's a lot going on in documents. That means there's a lot for us to see (and need to see) in these things when we read them. We'll start by taking a look at reading as a corporate lawyer, and then we'll turn to writing.

Expert Reading

Scholars have studied legal reading. They've compared how experienced lawyers and 1Ls read legal texts. They've also studied how graduate students from other disciplines read legal documents.

Some of the findings are obvious. Experts do better than novices, even really smart novices. "Domain knowledge," knowledge of the subject matter or discipline, is the most critical factor affecting comprehension. A bank lawyer reads credit agreements in a more sophisticated way than, say, a geologist or an employment lawyer.

No surprise there. Domain knowledge comes with experience and study.

Other observations from the scholarly literature are of more immediate interest.

First, expert readers read for a purpose. They are immersed in business context. They know why they're reading and, to that end, seek out relevant information. They don't necessarily start reading on page 1, and they don't necessarily limit their reading to the document in front of them; ancillary may become primary pretty quick.

Second, they are "involved" with the document. They jump between sections, scribble in the margins, re-read passages. They might even groan (or laugh) once in awhile.

Third, they understand the terminology, conventions, and organizational structure of the document. They know how the document works, the functionality of the various components, and how those components relate to one another. That knowledge — whether it's of a contract, board resolution, SEC filing, statute, or judicial opinion — helps them read more efficiently and purposively.

(That's why learning vocab and characteristic organizational schemes and conventions is so useful; it helps build fluidity with the material.)

Fourth, experts engage with documents in multiple ways.

Just as you did with casebooks, experts underline, highlight, and summarize text in an effort to understand what it says.

They monitor their own comprehension. They imagine scenarios, make speculations, and try to figure things out. They evaluate the document as they get deeper into it. They have views about the content and how it's expressed.

As with staring at a visual, experts talk to themselves all the time, asking questions ("what does this mean?") and expressing opinions ("why did they do it that way?"... or sometimes, on a bad day, "why did *we* do it this way?) as they work through the document.

Expert lawyer reading is an active, self-aware, almost physical process. Remember: reading is a fundamental activity of the job.

Expert lawyer reading is an engaged, self-aware process.

SEEK	DECODE	MOVE	SUMMARIZE	QUESTION	EVALUATE
· Reads for a concrete purpose · Seeks out relevant information · Actively engages with text	· Recognizes words · Knows how terminology works	· Knows organization and structure of document · Understands components and relationships between components · Understands conventions used in document	· Underlines, highlights, summarizes, and paraphrases text · Tries to understand what text is about	· Monitors understanding of text by asking questions, making predictions, and hypothesizing · Moves back and forth while reading · Monitors comprehension difficulties and works to address them	· Evaluates and forms opinions about document · Criticizes both ideas expressed and quality of expression

motivation   mechanics   strategies (talking to yourself)

Layered Reading

Another way to come at it: think about all the things going on in a document, all the things you need to see. Consider reading legal products multiple times for multiple purposes.

For example, read for substance. What's going on here? Transaction structure? Flow of money? Asset ownership? Risk allocations? Behavioral rules? Decision-making processes? Conflicts with other agreements? Exit rights?

Read for impact and implications. If we do this, what's the operational impact? Can we live with it? Too constraining commercially? Burdensome administratively? Accounting implications? Perception by potential readers such as regulators, employees, customers, competitors, media, auditors? (In-house lawyers are particularly attuned to these impact questions.)

Read for legal craft. Does this provision achieve the intended legal result? Is it reflective of underlying law? Does the document comply with technical requirements? Is it logically organized? Is it consistent with the related documents? Is it internally consistent?

Read for technical execution. Does it use defined terms consistently? Are the cross-references accurate? Is the table of contents accurate? Are there typos? Is it aesthetically appealing?

Remember, you're not just looking for information. You're evaluating a product across multiple dimensions.

You know about the potency of legal documents, their blend of business and law, their functionality and consequences. You're aware of longevity, visibility, and the reality of multiple readers. You know about technical complexity. You understand that quality expectations are high. You know there can be a lot happening in these things.

Your task when reading is to see as much and as far as you can. And, frankly, it's impossible to see everything in one pass. Instead, think (again) about layers, and try to read one layer at a time.

If you can, take a break between phases. You'll find that you can see more. And, especially with giant contracts and other big documents, print them out. It can be very challenging to see what you need to see by scrolling through a big document on a computer. You'll find things in a printed document that can easily be missed on a screen.

Being mindful of reading as a skill and discipline, and thinking about a work-product as a product, can be a useful way of approaching this aspect of our trade. Reading this way is like sketching; it can help you see relationships and other features you may otherwise have missed. As you gain more experience, you'll find that you'll see more, and see it faster.

Consider reading legal documents multiple times for multiple purposes.

SUBSTANCE

- Transaction structure
- Flow of value
- Asset ownership
- Risk allocations
- Behavioral rules
- Project plan
- Events requiring action or permitting exit
- Conflicts with other agreements
- Decision-making process

IMPACT

- Operational impact
- Accounting implications
- Disclosure consequences
- Perception by potential readers (parties, employees, auditors, investors, competitors, regulators, media, litigants, judges, juries)
- Anticipation of audit, investigation, or litigation
- Divergence from convention or past practice
- Precedent-setting implications
- Evidentiary implications

LEGAL CRAFT

- Achievement of intended legal results
- Reflective of underlying law (consistency/contracting out)
- Logical/natural design and organization
- Document efficiency
- Compliance with requirements relating to form and content
- Internal consistency (within itself and with related documents)
- Clarity/accessibility/usability
- Writing quality

TECHNICAL EXECUTION

- Consistent and accurate use of defined terms
- Accuracy of cross-references
- Consistency between section captions and content
- Correct citation and format
- Accuracy of table of contents
- Lack of typographical errors
- Aesthetic quality

Reverse Architecture

Let's dig into a stack of documents.

In both advisory and planning situations, it's common for the client to have in place a bunch of documents. Or you may be doing due diligence on a transaction and find yourself in a data room with lots of files. Or you may be asked to get up to speed on a project financing or product commercialization arrangement where the definitive agreement,

ancillary agreements, and related materials fill three binders.

Part of the task is simply to figure out what's there. What is all this stuff? How do these documents relate to one another? What's covered where?

Think about doing some high-level "reverse architecture."

Make a little drawing identifying the key documents. Try to note the core function of each doc, and how each piece fits together. See if you can follow the action. Look for overlaps, inconsistencies, and inefficiencies. Jot down what you see, and the questions you have.

You'll end up with a useful tool for follow-up investigation and advice development.

Figure out how the documents
relate to one another.

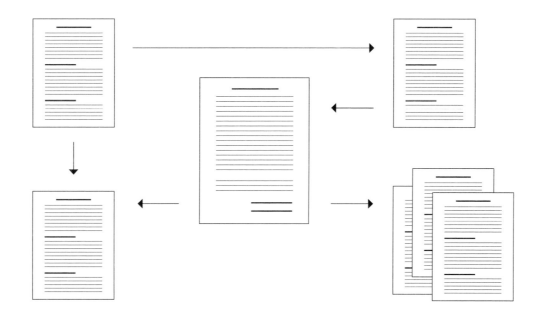

Understanding the Document

Some individual documents can be pretty challenging to understand. Common sense and awareness of basic organizational schemes and conventions will help you get a handle at a high level, but, to really understand and work with the document, you need to dig deeper.

Especially if it's really long.

You can use a visual to help figure things out.

A contract, for example, may contemplate a variety of asset and information flows. It may set out a detailed plan for the relationship, and provide for an elaborate set of responses to the occurrence of specified contingencies. It may set out multiple financial and operating measurement periods. A timeline can be quite useful here; it can help you see the key events and timeframes.

Or think about a drug deal. Imagine a small company with a great idea and a big pharmaceutical company with scientific, regulatory, manufacturing, and marketing might. They plan to work together to get from experiment in the lab to approved drug in the U.S., European, and Japanese markets.

That's a rather serious undertaking. Not surprisingly, these commercialization agreements are long and complex. They include development plans, decision-making arrangements, and rules relating to IP ownership, regulatory filings, manufacturing, marketing, production, and liability matters.

The economics are tied to the achievement of specified milestones. There may be different terms for different territories, and different economics depending on the presence of a competitive product in the territory.

Might need to take an aspirin after dealing with one of those, huh?

The reality is that it may be practically impossible to comprehend a document (or explain it to a client) without making a sketch or other simplifying representation. You need a tool for breaking the thing down. Such a piece may also become the basis for a cheat sheet or other implementation piece that will be wonderfully helpful for the client.

It may be practically impossible to comprehend a document without a simplifying representation.

FROM LAB TO MARKETPLACE

A: Small company
B: Big pharmaceutical company

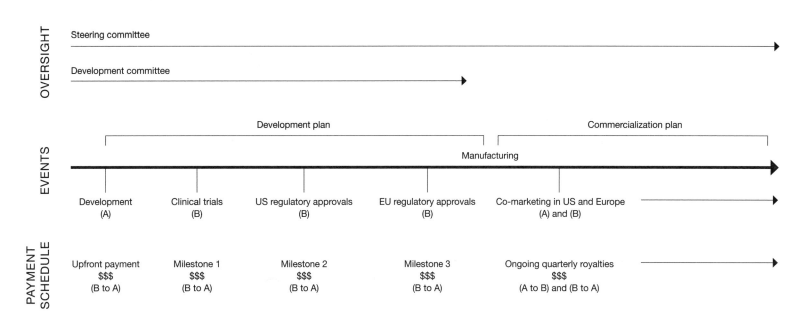

Making New Documents

Let's move from engaging with existing documents to creating something new.

In every situation, whether it's an advisory or a transactional setting, we have to figure out what to make for the client.

What we make will be a function of the situation or deal structure. It's often more than one piece, as we saw with the definitive and ancillary agreements from transaction planning. In some cases, the package will reflect legal requirements and practice conventions. In

advisory and other cases, we may just need to make it up.

So: what kind of documents do we make? And how do they relate to each other?

We need a plan. We need a document architecture.

A simple drawing may help.

Step back and think about what you can do to help the client. Figure out the work, legal and otherwise, you need to get done with the docs. Sketch out the possible pieces. Figure out what gets covered in what piece.

If there's a main document — say, a definitive purchase agreement, or a big advice piece — maybe make that box bigger, to convey its primacy, and the time required to produce it.

Depending on the situation, the plan may emerge very quickly, or it may evolve over time as you get deeper into the work.

Be sure not to forget the communication documents — the transmittal e-mail, memo, or other product that will orient the client or other recipient to the other materials you prepared. Those are what the recipient sees first, they're really important, and they take time to do well.

A simple visual can help you figure out what to make for the client.

Loan agreement
(operative)

Security agreement
(operative)

Guarantee
(operative)

Compliance checklist
(implementation)

Transmittal memo
(communication)

Using Precedents and Forms

We often use forms and "precedent" documents as the base, or at least the inspiration, for our products.

Our precedents are different than law school precedents; no *International Shoe* or stare decisis for us. Precedents here just means documents used in prior comparable transactions.

Precedents and law firm and other model forms are great. They're low cost and reflect solutions developed over time and tested in the marketplace. You can think of them as intellectual property of your firm. Partners may point you to precedents and forms and in any case will ask you about what you used in putting together the draft.

Sometimes it helps to sketch out, really quickly, your plan on how to use those materials. Identify the documents from which you'll borrow. If you're just adapting specific sections, call them out.

When you do borrow, be sure to be mindful of consistency and accuracy. It's easy when adapting text to have substantive, terminology, and consistency problems.

For example, the precedent may shade the substance in favor of one party or the other, or the substance may be shaky in view of recent caselaw. The borrowed language may include defined terms or mentions of topics that are not relevant to your document. The precedent or form may follow different conventions on language ("will" vs. "shall"), punctuation (Oxford comma), or emphasis (underling or italicizing a phrase such as "provided, however.")

And, above all, be sure to scrub the borrowed text for party names or other identifying facts; those can be easily missed, and it's bad news when they appear in your draft.

Forms are inputs, not outputs. Even though they may look great, you still need to engage closely with them and make sure to fit them to your facts, and to your overall document set.

Remember, too, that precedents reflect negotiated outcomes, and forms aren't perfect. They need to evolve over time to reflect legal, market, and other developments. If you see a mistake, or don't understand something, or see an opportunity for improvement, be sure to speak up.

Dissenting opinions are needed now and then when it comes to these precedents.

Precedents and forms are great — but be sure to shape them to your facts.

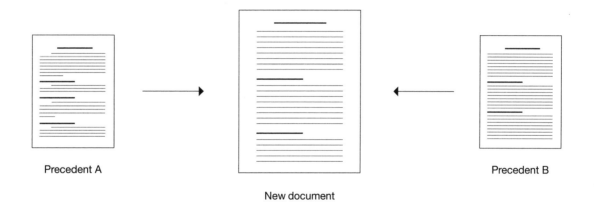

Precedent A

New document

Precedent B

Creating a New Document

Occasionally we're on our own and need to create documents that differ markedly from forms or precedents. Or maybe we're repairing a bad document by breaking it down and starting over.

Start by listing out what you want to cover. Think about the work you want to do. Figure out what you want to accomplish with the document.

A simple list of provisions or subject matters is fine. Try to organize the items on that list into a manageable number of categories. An outline helps with that bucketing process.

But, instead of a classic top-to-bottom outline, try horizontal. Put the categories on top and the topics of individual sections or provisions underneath.

This format may make it easier to experiment and come up with a logical organizational scheme and sequencing — which can be a deceptively challenging exercise when you're working from scratch or incorporating an unusual feature into a base document. It may help you see the flow, and the story being told in the document; somehow, it makes it easier to see "overallness."

A similar horizontal approach is useful when you're developing a presentation or discussion document (often called a "deck"), where you really are trying to tell a story, and there may not be good precedents available. Think of storyboards used in creating a film or animation as a model. The logic, the key points and themes, the progression from beginning to end, are all in front of you.

A whiteboard or tablet is great for this sort of thing, especially when you're working with a colleague — it makes it easy to point, explain, and adjust as you together plan the document.

For a discussion deck, try storyboarding.
For a contract, try a horizontal outline.
Both help you see the flow, from beginning to end.

STORYBOARD

HORIZONTAL OUTLINE

BUCKET 1   BUCKET 2   BUCKET 3   BUCKET 4

Changing the Document

Recall that document work is group work. You're likely to have multiple readers of your draft. No doubt they will have plenty of comments. That's just the nature of the game.

Be prepared for mysterious terminology when you get those comments.

A partner may direct you to make a "global change" or say that you need to "conform that to the definitive agreement." She might also say that she'll be giving you a couple of "riders," and finish by instructing you to send her a "cumulative redline" to review before you put together the "execution copy," which the parties will sign "in counterparts."

Say what?

All this is standard stuff in the trade.

A "global change" is typically a terminology thing; change "Smith" to "Jones" everywhere in all the documents. But don't just rely on the find-and-replace function. You will be embarrassed if you do. Misspellings, possessives, capitalization, use of a word in different contexts, text borrowed from a precedent… all can create problems if you just replace a word without checking.

A "conforming change" is more substantive. A concept or a characterization may appear in various forms in multiple places in a document or in multiple related documents. If the concept changes, you need to address the change in all of those places.

This is not brain-dead work; the ripple effects of a refinement can be subtle, and it's your job to find and fix them.

A "rider" is simply a standalone insert.

"Redlines" are probably familiar from the track changes function in Microsoft Word. A redline is a document that shows the changes from the prior draft. A "cumulative redline" is just what it sounds like; it shows all the changes, through multiple revisions, from the original to the current draft. Partners may want to see redlines along the way ("interim redlines") so they can see how the document is shaping up as a result of negotiation and additional work.

"Execution copy" refers to the final, fully-agreed contract document. This is the version that the parties will sign ("execute"); it's the real deal. The little header that says "draft" is removed, and actual dates, numbers, and names are filled in. Oftentimes, these docs have an "Execution Copy" legend in the header on the first page.

And "counterparts?" Parties to a contact are often in different locations and don't sign a single signature page. Instead, as contemplated by a common boilerplate provision, they sign separate "counterpart" sig pages, which are combined to make for a fully-executed contract.

One other note: you'll want to take opportunities to sharpen up your word processing skills. Carpenters use hammers, levels, and saws; we use Microsoft Word. Same idea.

A concept changes, and you're told to conform the docs.

It has an impact in this section.

Here, too: an entire article needs to drop out.

The termination rules need to be adjusted.

And it affects several ancillary docs as well.

When you're done, you do a redline.

Tate sit quos dolup tatus, cuptatia cul faceptam que prere, quam qui ut qui vent. Les dolupta

Tate sit quos dolup tatus, cuptatia cul exerum que natiam ideliquis enderch illorios. Les dolupta

There are counterpart signature pages.

x ___Alice___
Alice

x _____
John

x _____
Alice

x ___John___
John

Checking the Document

The standards for execution of a legal product are really, really high. That should be no surprise given their consequentiality, longevity, visibility, and cost.

That means you need to get everything right.

Documents, as we've seen, may be intensely technical in nature, with lots of defined terms and cross-references. You may want to create a little checklist calling out these sorts of items (and other easy things to mess up, like orphan lines and section numbering), and then discipline yourself to march through the list when you near completion of a document.

It seems silly, but it works, and you certainly don't want clients or senior colleagues to find such mistakes before you do. The reality is that colleagues, clients, and counterparties will make judgments about your competence based on the quality of the execution. You don't want your substantive advice questioned, or your reputation damaged, because of sloppy work.

The other thing is, you have to nail this every time out. That can be challenging when you're tired, or stressed, or bored with looking at the same documents over and over. There's no choice; you just have to maintain your edge. That's what pros do.

Think about a trip to the dentist for a routine filling. Do you think the dentist is fired up about fixing your cavity? She's only done this procedure a thousand times. But, don't you expect your dentist to do a great job, whether she's excited or not? To get it perfect? Long-lasting and no rough edges?

Same deal here. Professionals execute at a professional level, every time out. For a lawyer, that includes tight documents.

So be sure to figure out what works for you to help you see the littlest picture as well as the big, and stick to it.

PROOFREADING CHECKLIST

☐ Does the document have page numbers?

☐ Are defined terms properly capitalized, actually defined, and used consistently when appropriate?

☐ Do cross-references match the correct section?

☐ Do section and paragraph captions reflect the related text?

☐ Are section captions kept with related text (no orphan captions)?

☐ Are there no orphan lines?

☐ Does the document have the right header/footer?

☐ Are all of the headers/footers consistent across all of the documents?

☐ Do the numbers or letters on any numbered document reflect the actual ordering?

☐ Have you removed placeholders (e.g., brackets) and internal comments?

☐ Have you used consistent margins?

☐ Have you run a spellcheck?

☐ Have you checked for punctuation?

☐ Did you use "print preview" to check overall document appearance?

Building Documents

Construction is a good way of thinking about transactional work. It's also a good way of thinking about documents.

Documents get built, not written. You don't stare out the window and wait for the commercial lease muse to arrive.

Instead, you take parts, you put things together, and you polish it up.

So rather than sitting down and expecting the words to flow, think about the document architecture, do a rough sketch, and head for the parts room.

Maybe there's a good form. If not, try just hacking things together — create a shell, grab provisions from precedents, and drop them in.

For contracts, if you don't have a model on point, think about starting at each end — the semi-standardized intro in the front and boilerplate and sig pages in the back — and then working in toward the middle from each side. Sort of like how they built the transcontinental railroad.

This process gets you going, and it just feels better to start editing sooner rather than later. You'll have a lot of refining to do, to make sure concepts, terminology, and language are consistent, and you'll have free drafting to do, but you get to a tangible product pretty quickly.

It's like building a house. Once the frame is up, you can really see and get a feel for the place. You know you're well underway.

Documents get built,
not written.

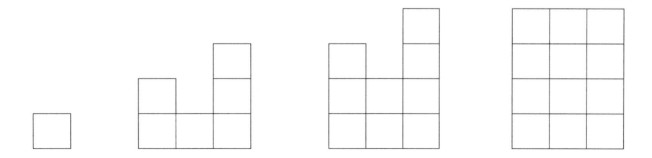

Looking and Seeing, Fast

These observations about engaged reading and document construction in many ways reflect what we've been discussing throughout this book.

They're another manifestation of the analytical, step-by-step character of the work that we saw in advice development and deal planning.

They're a natural counterpart to the reality and richness of legal documents.

They're consistent with how we lawyers look at the world and, in that lawyer way, evaluate what we see on multiple levels from multiple points of view, adding layers as we move along.

Here, the world is a document. We look at it and see a lot.

A way to think about this is to consider how an experienced physician or mechanic can take a quick look at something — a wound, an ear

canal, a brake assembly — and immediately identify the problem, explain the implications, describe the fix, and then do the repair. It's like a miracle.

That's what experienced corporate lawyers can do when they read a legal document. They understand the terminology, know how the pieces fit together, see the work the document is doing, understand why it is doing that work, assess the quality, recognize the consequences of a change in concept or language, and come up with improvements. If they need to keep it in the shop or run some tests, they do, to make sure they get it right.

Building that facility and speed is the goal (because, among other things, of the cost of legal services and the need to work efficiently in view of all those projects on your plate). That's why awareness of document functionality, consequences, organizational schemes,

conventions, and other characteristics is so useful. You know what to look for, you know where to look, and you know how to put the parts together.

It's also why visuals and checklists can be helpful.

Visuals help you understand the substance of a complex document, and give you a tangible vehicle for adding layers as you think about the influences on, and implications of, a document. They're also useful tools for document architecture and outlining.

Checklists are great because it's hard to remember everything you need to inspect, especially when you're tired and juggling multiple projects. Checklists are basic quality control tools in lots of fields. If they're good enough for pilots and surgeons, they're probably good enough for us, too.

This is Our Craft

Another way to think about this is by returning to the construction analogy and contemplating the craft nature of our job, the fact that we do skilled technical work.

We make products. Our products, like cabinets made by a carpenter, need to be functional for the user. The cabinet needs to hold dishes, and the document needs to license the trademark.

The product has to have structural integrity. The cabinet shouldn't collapse when you fill up the drawers, and the contract should stand up if the relationship comes under pressure.

And the product has to be aesthetically appealing and built in the right way. A scratch on the cabinet top or inconsistent margins in the document may not diminish functionality, but who's going to be happy with that?

For some, the notion of building a product has resonance and appeal, and can be a way of

tempering, at least a little, the grind-it-out nature of billable hour expectations. Like the carpenter, we need to understand how the product works, what makes for a good product, and how to construct the product.

You can think of what we do (or should do) as bringing to the work the imagination, discipline, and dedication to quality that characterizes a master craftsperson.

Folks are sometimes surprised by how gratifying it can be to move from a client conversation and pile of materials to a whiteboard to a shell to a messy half-baked draft to a thoughtful and polished work-product.

We take the wood and end up with a useful, solidly-built, and handsome cabinet. Not a bad day's work.

Final Thoughts: Working with our Products

- Figure out what's in front of you

- Figure out the document architecture

- Find relevant precedents and models

- Get started by grabbing parts and framing it out

- Work through comments closely and patiently

- Read multiple times for multiple purposes

- Make it perfect

7 / Preparing for a Board Meeting

In both advisory and deal situations, lawyers advise clients about the need and process for formal board action. This chapter offers ideas for how to approach such assignments.

You recall our central actor, the corporation.

In Corporations or Business Associations, you learned about corporate governance. You learned about the basic governance structure (board of directors, board committees, officers) and about the role of the board. You read cases involving the fiduciary duties of care and loyalty.

As a corporate lawyer, you help design governance arrangements, and you help boards carry out those duties. As a deal lawyer, you work with boards to obtain their approval of a transaction. Indeed, it's common, in both advisory and deal settings, for a partner to direct an associate to "put together what we need for the board."

A good way to think about this work (and, for that matter, a lot of legal work) is that you are a process designer. You help facilitate decisions. You develop information, shape the meeting plan, and document outcomes. You need to figure out and create a plan to get folks from proposal to approved corporate action. And you need to make sure they get there in a manner reflective of applicable legal principles.

In effect, you're writing a script. This chapter provides some suggestions for getting started.

Sources and Influences

Let's begin by refreshing ourselves on the underlying law.

You no doubt used a statutory supplement in your Corporations class. It probably contained the Delaware General Corporation Law and some other state statutes, excerpts from the federal securities laws, stock exchange listing standards, and other authorities.

Those supplements nicely capture a central fact about corporate governance and decision-making: there are plenty of rules and influences. The relevant state corporation law is the core; it tells us about big things like mergers and small things like meeting notice mechanics.

The other sources are based in both law and private ordering.

The federal securities laws and stock exchange listing requirements cover relevant ground, including director independence and board committee composition and responsibilities.

Judicial opinions shape board practices; think about the huge body of Delaware law regarding board actions in merger and other settings.

Compliance requirements and criminal sentencing guidelines influence risk management and board oversight activities.

On the market side, contract terms — such as those in an investors' rights or a stockholders' agreement — may affect board composition, information access, approval rights, and other matters. Proxy advisors publish governance standards. Big mutual funds adopt voting guidelines. Activist investors push for changes in board practices.

And, of course, clients make numerous decisions about their own arrangements: board size, board terms, board composition goals, committee structure, management delegations, and so on.

Governance arrangements (and associated documents) reflect multiple influences. Even before you start working through the client's materials, you will already be well underway with understanding them: you go in knowing there's a lot of legal and management stuff going on underneath.

Governance arrangements reflect
multiple legal, market, and client influences.

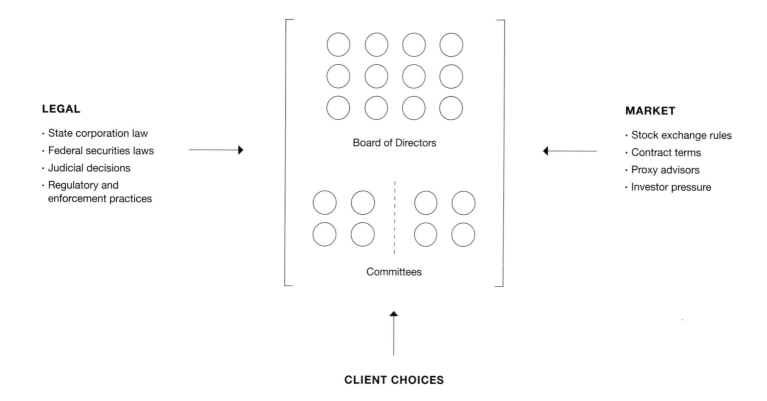

LEGAL

· State corporation law
· Federal securities laws
· Judicial decisions
· Regulatory and
  enforcement practices

Board of Directors

Committees

MARKET

· Stock exchange rules
· Contract terms
· Proxy advisors
· Investor pressure

CLIENT CHOICES

Governance Documents

As for those documents:

There are the articles (or certificate) of incorporation, the organic document of the corporation. Common and preferred stock terms are set out here.

There are the bylaws, which provide the governance framework. Bylaws deal with the mechanics of board and stockholder meetings, director elections, board committees, officers, and director indemnification.

There are charters for each board committee, short documents which typically cover committee composition, responsibilities, and administration. Stock exchange requirements for committee functions are reflected in these charters.

There are often separate policies relating to related party transactions, director independence, director stock ownership, and similar matters.

Public companies maintain governance guidelines covering director qualification standards, responsibilities, compensation, orientation, continuing education, and self-evaluation.

Public and other companies have codes of ethics addressing topics such as conflicts of interest, corporate opportunity, confidentiality, fair dealing, protection of corporate assets, corruption, and reporting of illegal or unethical behavior. A company may have such a code focused on directors and executive officers, and a much broader "code of business conduct" applicable across the business.

There may be a stockholders' agreement, credit agreement, or other contract that includes provisions relating to governance arrangements, transactions with affiliates, and approvals of specified actions.

Boards may use practical tools such as calendars, self-assessment questionnaires, and orientation materials to help guide and evaluate their work.

Directors typically receive extensive reading materials ("board books") before board and committee meetings.

Boards and committees adopt resolutions and keep minutes of their meetings. Minutes are important; as we'll see, they're the official record of board action.

Lots of docs. Depending on the nature of the matter up for review, you may need to work your way through a variety of sources.

(Good news: as with contracts and other legal documents, you'll see a lot of commonality in how companies put together these materials, and over time, you'll be able to work through the review in a pretty efficient way.)

DOCUMENT	CONTENT	DOCUMENT	CONTENT
Articles (or certificate) of incorporation	Corporate name, common and preferred stock terms, director liability	Governance guidelines (public companies)	Director qualification standards and responsibilities, compensation, orientation, continuing education, and self-evaluation
Bylaws	Mechanics of board and stockholder meetings, director elections, board committees, and director indemnification	Codes of ethics and business conduct	Conflicts of interest, corporate opportunity, confidentiality, and other matters
Charters (board committee)	Committee composition, responsibilities, and administration	Calendars / self-assessment questionnaires / orientation materials	Planning, performance evaluation, education
Policies	Related party transactions, director independence, and similar matters	Board books	Information about matters to be considered at meeting
Contracts	Governance arrangements and transaction approvals	Resolutions / minutes	Deliberations and actions at meetings

Figuring Out What's Needed

You now have a stack of documents. It's time to figure out what specifically we need to do to get the deal approved. We need to ask some basic questions.

What is the subject matter of the decision?

Different subject matters may be addressed by different authorities and be subject to different requirements. Think about a related party situation; we may need to deal with both a statute and an internal policy. Or the statute, bylaws or contract may require more than a standard majority vote on certain matters.

Who needs to approve it?

Different subject matters may have different decision makers. A committee may need to review. A related party situation may require a vote of disinterested directors. A stockholders' agreement may require us to obtain approval from an investor. As always, time is a concern; it will take longer to get the full board to sign off versus a committee.

What are the standards for approval?

Different decisions may have different approval prerequisites. An affirmative decision may, for example, require certain factual findings or policy conclusions by the board. In order to establish the basis for those conclusions, in some matters we may want careful meeting scripting in line with fiduciary duty and litigation anticipation considerations.

What are the mechanics for approval?

Mechanics are essential to proper meeting execution. There are legal fundamentals such as appropriate notice of a meeting or the presence of a quorum at the meeting.

You get the idea.

This is yet another logical, layered inquiry, another form of advice development and project planning. You need to look, label, examine relevant materials, figure out the plan, and identify what we need to make to carry out the plan. You just need to march through it.

A drawing can be useful here. You can call out relevant underlying docs, sketch out the steps required under the docs, note relevant timelines, and identify needed information and actions. It's like a mini-version of a transaction plan: actions, timing, documents.

Board meeting planning is another
logical, look-and-label, layered inquiry.

WHAT ———————▶ **WHO** ———————▶ **STANDARDS** ———————▶ **MECHANICS**

What is the
subject matter of
the decision?

Who needs to
approve it?

What are
the standards
for approval?

What are
the mechanics
for approval?

Information for the Board

You've gotten a feel now for process. There's a related question: what information does the decision-maker need?

This isn't just an administrative matter; this is core legal.

The fiduciary duty of care requires directors to be reasonably informed of relevant facts when making a decision. Directors are entitled to rely upon information provided by management and by company advisors such as investment bankers and lawyers. Materials provided to a board are important pieces of evidence should the decision later be challenged. You're creating the record here.

Besides, it's just smart to give the senior leadership group solid and complete information, right? You want them to make a good decision.

So what do we need to cover and include in the board book?

Think business first, as your client will; management will be deeply involved and you'll work closely with them in creating the board materials. What should the board be thinking about? Strategic fit? Financial impact? Risk? Internal capacity? Corporate reputation? Tax consequences? Lessons learned from the last time out?

Think time and project management again: these materials will go through multiple levels of review. The CEO and other senior managers will be deeply attuned to how information is presented to the board (their boss), and materials will need to be sent out to the directors well in advance of the meeting. That lead time reflects not only practical but also duty of care considerations; the board should have meaningful time to study the background materials.

Lawyers can play an important role here.

We're good information managers.

We do document architecture, figuring out what pieces we need to do what work. We're disciplined in generating, verifying, and summarizing information. We pay more attention than most to accuracy and consistency.

Moreover, we know we need to study materials not only with a view to the immediate readership (directors) but also to potential future readers. We know we need to look ahead, to use our imagination and think about how these materials will appear in other (and probably less cheerful) settings.

Preparation of board materials is also an example of the importance of lawyer facility with language.

We need to consider and accommodate a variety of business, legal, practical, and political considerations. And we need to shape them in a way that works for busy and intense people.

The board book is a management
resource that's pretty important from
a legal point of view, too.

INFORMATION

· Strategic fit
· Financial impact
· Risk
· Internal capacity
· Reputational impact
· Tax consequences
· Prior experiences

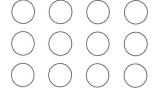

BOARD OF DIRECTORS

· Duty of care
· Reliance on experts
· Building the record

Meeting Activity

You may not get to attend the board or committee meeting. But you'll be there, because your homework — the process you developed — will help shape the session.

Does the board need to make factual findings? Do we need any individual directors to recuse themselves on certain matters? Do we need a super-majority vote for approval? Do we need to allow time for a presentation by a financial advisor? Do we need a report from a board committee? You will have figured all this out and advised the client accordingly.

Your advice on such matters goes into the plan for the meeting. It's reflected in an agenda prepared for the chair of the board and general counsel. The agenda will also remind the chair to confirm that a quorum exists, that directors calling in can hear everyone, and satisfaction of other meeting mechanics requirements.

The board materials you helped prepare will prompt discussion and questions. That's good, from a fiduciary point of view. If you and your colleagues on the business side have done their job, you will have anticipated questions

and reflected them in the materials, which contributes to a productive discussion. That also makes management look good (which is always good).

When the discussion concludes, the proposed resolutions you drafted (more to follow) will be adopted by the board and reflect their formal approval.

You're just about there.

The meeting plan will drive meeting activity (and development of the record).

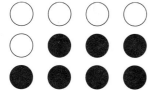

- Mechanics (such as a quorum)

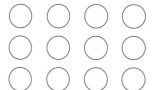

- Presentations
- Discussions
- Deliberations
- Mechanics (such as recusal)

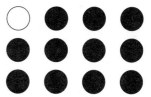

- Mechanics (such as approval levels)
- Findings
- Decision

Minutes and Resolutions

There's one other thing to do. Somebody needs to prepare the minutes for the meeting.

Minutes are important. They are required by statute, and they are evidence. Indeed, in California, by statute board minutes are "prima facie evidence of … the due holding of such meeting and of the matters stated therein."

Minutes get a lot of work done. They identify attendees and whether they are attending or participating by phone. They confirm the existence of a quorum. They note presenters and participation of non-director attendees such as bankers. This is useful information to have in the record.

Most importantly, minutes include reporting about the discussions and actions taken at the meeting. They tell the story of the decision and are the record of the deliberations; they help document the exercise of care and judgment by the board.

Different organizations and different lawyers have different views about the level of detail to be contained in board minutes. Some like a lot and some like a little. Different situations may call for different approaches; approval of a merger is a tad more sensitive than, say, the annual election of assistant secretaries.

You need to understand client and partner practices and preferences, and pay attention to context.

Minutes also recite formal resolutions adopted by a board to approve a transaction or other action such as the creation of a board committee. Typically, proposed resolutions are included in the board book, and then are sometimes tweaked in the meeting at the time of adoption.

You'll draft the resolutions. These typically are pretty old-fashioned documents, using a "whereas, whereas, now let it be resolved" style. But they're great. You can use them to reflect awareness and compliance with relevant statutory and bylaw requirements ("whereas, pursuant to Section 141(f)…"), establish predicates ("whereas, the Committee reviewed and recommended…"), and document that the board jumped through the necessary hoops ("whereas, Ms. Smith recused herself and did not participate in the discussion").

You can, in short, use them as both a tool for documenting the homework and for building the record in a manner favorable to your client. This is an opportunity and responsibility of general importance and of critical importance in public company M&A and executive compensation situations.

And, very practically, you can use them to facilitate future actions by delegating authority to officers to approve contract amendments, sign related documents, and the like.

Minutes and resolutions reflect the functionality, longevity, and potential visibility of legal documents; they get work done and, as we'll see, somebody may be reading these things down the road.

So remember: think ahead — and think as a defense lawyer. Better yet, think as a plaintiff's lawyer, too.

Minutes and resolutions reflect the functionality, longevity, and visibility of legal documents.

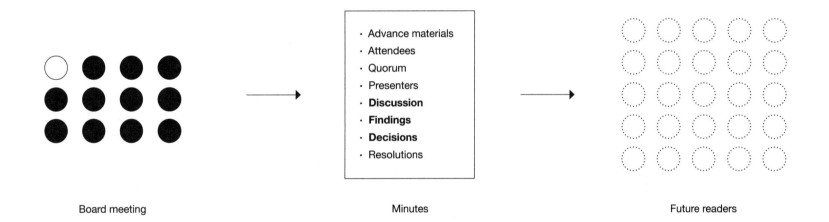

Board meeting

- Advance materials
- Attendees
- Quorum
- Presenters
- **Discussion**
- **Findings**
- **Decisions**
- Resolutions

Minutes

Future readers

Why Pay Attention

It's important to pay close attention to board meeting and other governance work because others will be paying attention.

Board members, senior executives, and the general counsel of your client see your work. Enough said.

Auditors review board minutes as part of the annual audit process because minutes may contain information relevant both to the financial statements and to the auditor's assessment of internal corporate processes.

Transaction parties review board materials as part of the due diligence for an acquisition or financing. They also review bylaws, committee charters, and resolutions prior to closing in order to confirm proper approval of the transaction.

You do not, repeat do not, want the associate on the other side of the deal to give you a hard time about your resolutions. Imagine having to call the partner or client and tell them that,

by reason of your mistake, the other side is demanding that the client have another board meeting and adopt new resolutions approving the deal. Not good.

Your client will make representations and warranties in contracts about governance arrangements and board approvals. Client officers will make certifications about these matters in closing certificates.

Your firm may give a formal opinion about the client's governance arrangements and transaction approval actions. Partners like to see things buttoned up pretty tightly in opinion-giving settings.

You may need to submit board books and other materials to regulators as part of a transaction review. That's what happens with the antitrust agencies in connection with certain acquisition transactions; they want to see how management (internally) views the proposed deal.

Your client, if it's public, will file its articles and bylaws as exhibits to SEC filings, post its committee charters, governance guidelines, key policies, and code of conduct on its website, and report extensively on governance arrangements and execution in its proxy statement. If it's engaged in a merger, the disclosure document will report on the board process and deliberations about the deal.

Your client, if it's involved in litigation, may need to produce board materials, including both board books and minutes, as well as related drafts, notes, and e-mails, in discovery.

And on and on and on.

Governance execution is visible and subject to scrutiny. Understand that errors eventually will be found, and know that it's no fun if they are. Diligence, thoughtfulness, and close reading — all good lawyer values and qualities — are really important here.

Process is Us

Preparing the plan for a board meeting is an example of the process design and information management we do all the time as lawyers.

We have to take into account relevant influences and constraints, including legal requirements.

We have to anticipate future reviewers and critics of the process.

We have to create materials for those involved in the process to study before the meeting.

We have to identify needed actions by the actors at the meeting, from presentations to voting.

We have to make sure stage directions are clear, including such things as voting requirements and the need for specific findings.

And we have to document the performance.

It's script writing in a context where we want neither comedy nor drama. We just want a smooth, manageable, and airtight process that will stand up over time.

Final Thoughts: Preparing for a Board Meeting

- Gather the documents
- Determine the subject matter of the decision
- Determine who needs to approve it
- Determine the standards for approval
- Determine the mechanics of approval
- Prepare the advance materials
  (with a view toward future readers)
- Write the meeting script
- Document the meeting discussion and outcomes
  (with a view toward future readers)

8 / Being Mindful of Litigation

We corporate lawyers decided not to be litigators. But we still need to be mindful of litigation. This chapter offers some ideas about what we can (and should) do.

Let's think about litigation for a moment.

The good news is that litigation is rare. The vast majority of things we work on do not end up in litigation.

But it does happen. Contracts are breached, financial disclosures are misleading, board decisions are flawed, deal terms are anti-competitive. Or at least someone alleges that they are.

Our core task as corporate lawyers is to help our clients be successful in their businesses. We help them make thoughtful decisions, engage in productive commercial relationships, and communicate accurately to their constituents.

We generally shake hands with the other side more than we shake fists at them, which is a great thing.

Part of our job, though, is to imagine the worst, to advise our clients about litigation considerations, and to do what we can to position the client favorably in case things go bad.

So, given that we may be dealing with interrogatories and depositions at some point, let's take a brief look at what we can do with our advice, work-products, and conduct. We'll see, among other things, that it's wise for corporate lawyers to learn evidence for reasons in addition to the bar exam.

Substance

The obvious place to begin is with an obvious statement.

We have to get the legal stuff right.

We study the business. We listen closely to the client; they know their products, suppliers, licensees, organization, market, and anxieties much better than we do. We do our best to reflect their knowledge and address their concerns in the advice and deliverable.

We do solid technical work. The contract we draft is clear. The terms of the contract are enforceable under applicable statutes and the latest caselaw. The provisions do what they need to do to protect the client's intellectual property, create a security interest, or otherwise achieve the desired legal status. The statements in the stock offering disclosure document are substantiated. The privacy policy reflects best practice principles.

Good legal work (or, in more relevant terms, non-flawed-and-weak legal work) helps in court, and it helps in negotiating a resolution before court.

Substance in some cases means process.

Think about the script you wrote for the board meeting; you focused on the identity of the decision-makers, the information and advice considered, the quality of deliberations, and the record of all of the above.

Process is important in a variety of settings. As we'll see in the next chapter, underwriters of securities offerings defending misrepresentation claims by investors rely on the thoroughness of their due diligence. Companies defending claims involving termination of long-standing commercial relationships rely on advance notice and transition measures. Employers defending wrongful termination claims rely on their performance review processes.

Good process design and management, in short, is good litigation prep.

Our technical work as corporate lawyers is exposed (and leveraged) in litigation. Diligent and careful legal work is central to winning, especially, as we hope, to winning on summary disposition before trial. "Failure to state a claim" and "no genuine dispute as to any material fact" are sweet poetry for us as well as for the litigators.

We have to get the legal stuff right.

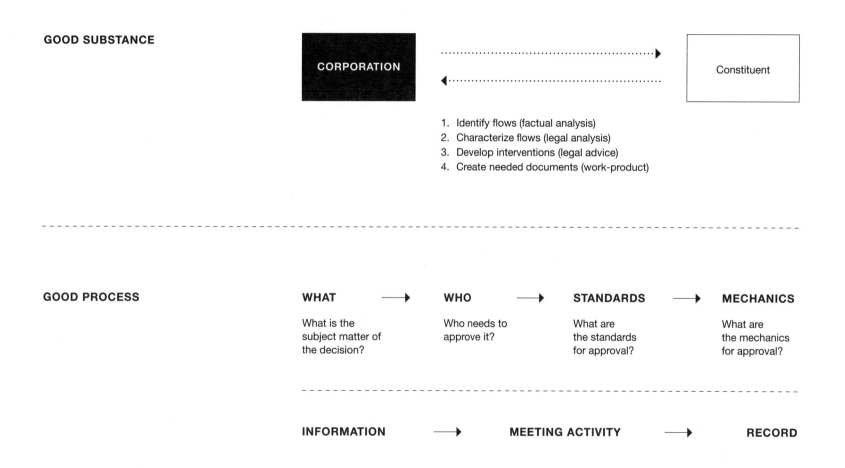

GOOD SUBSTANCE

CORPORATION

Constituent

1. Identify flows (factual analysis)
2. Characterize flows (legal analysis)
3. Develop interventions (legal advice)
4. Create needed documents (work-product)

GOOD PROCESS

WHAT →	WHO →	STANDARDS →	MECHANICS
What is the subject matter of the decision?	Who needs to approve it?	What are the standards for approval?	What are the mechanics for approval?

INFORMATION   →   MEETING ACTIVITY   →   RECORD

Plaintiff's Exhibit A

Our substantive legal work often centers on generating legal documents.

Documents are pretty important in lawsuits. They are discoverable and they have evidentiary value. They show up in all sorts of ways.

Documents "get litigated" in court. The meaning or effect of the document is at the center of the suit. That's why we have to nail it on the technical work.

That's also why litigators will tell you to read contract provisions and work through scenarios where you have to apply the rule or make the computation or follow the steps described in the provision. (Sketching can be really useful here. It's much like drawing a little picture to help figure out what's going on in a document when you first encounter it.) Come up with a situation and then see if the rule or formula or process you just devised actually works.

This can be a humbling exercise. And just wait until a dispute arises concerning a contractual provision you wrote X years ago.

Documents can influence their own interpretation by a court. Consider the entire agreement, waiver, severability, and governing law clauses in a contract.

Documents can influence how a dispute is resolved. Think about the indemnification, arbitration, mediation, injunctive relief, jurisdiction, and venue rules in a formal contract, employee handbook, or set of website terms.

Documents can shape the recovery in a lawsuit. Consider the damage limitation, exclusive remedy, and liquidated damage provisions in a contract, or the exculpatory provisions in a certificate of incorporation protecting directors from certain claims.

This litigation relevance reinforces why you should always study the boilerplate in a contract or other legal document. It's interesting that in the dysfunction of litigation we see so vividly the functionality of legal documents.

(Another suggestion: you might want to sign up for newsletters, webinars, and continuing education programs that report on case law developments in areas relevant to your practice. Bar sources and others also publish annual surveys of developments in various area of law. It may not be the most exciting reading, but it's a way of staying on top of how courts interpret standard contract clauses, and it's a way of learning about new statutes and early marketplace responses.)

CLASSIC CONTRACT COMPONENTS

COMPONENT	DESCRIPTION	DETAILS
Introduction	Gives the basics	· Name of agreement · Date of agreement · Parties · Nature of parties
Recitals	Tells the story of the deal	· Background · History · Objectives
Business terms	Describe the deal	· Asset · Price · Quantity · Payment · Time · Rights
Reps	Are about facts	· Reps are statements of facts · Warranties are promises that statements are true · Reps convey information and induce reliance
Covenants	Are promises about conduct	· Promise to do something (affirmative) · Promise not to do something (negative)
Conditions	Are prerequisites for performance	· If conditions not satisfied, then party not obligated to go forward

COMPONENT	DESCRIPTION	DETAILS
Indemnity	Is about protection	· Promise by which one protects another from a legal consequence of the conduct of a party or other person
Liability and remedies	Shapes litigation outcomes	· Limit recoverable damages · Limit (or provide) remedies
Termination	Is about the end game	· Sets out circumstances when one party can terminate contract or when contract terminates automatically · May also provide for consequences
Boilerplate	Is the (important) legal stuff in the back	· Contract interpretation including entire agreement, waiver, and severability · Amendment · Dispute resolution including tribunal and governing law
Signature blocks	Are about confirming agreement	· Identifies name of signatory · Identifies capacity of signatory · Satisfies statute of frauds
Schedules and exhibits	Do lots of things	· Set out business information · Respond to reps (exceptions, required disclosures) · Contain sample computations · Provide forms of ancillary and closing documents

Evidence is for Us, Too

Documents show up in other ways.

They can have independent significance (a contract) or be offered to prove a factual assertion (the board exercised due care) or be used to impeach a witness (the director's testimony is inconsistent with the e-mail).

Board minutes, as we saw, are evidence of what happened at the meeting. Training materials and compliance protocols may be evidence of reasonable care, or help defend against claims of willful or reckless activity, or provide a mitigating factor in corporate criminal sentencing.

On a more technical level, minutes and other corporate materials are likely considered business records or party admissions, admissible under exceptions to the hearsay rule. State law may speak to contract recitals; in California, for example, facts stated in contract recitals are presumed to be true, and there are other presumptions applicable to materials we see every day.

And more: contracts and other documents can contain admissions. Language in client communications and contracts can influence the availability of attorney-client privilege. Evidence principles relating to authentication,

best evidence, and so on may come into play — which is one of the many reasons you want to be punctilious about dating drafts and identifying their source.

If you're thoughtful about these things, if you take advantage of document functionality and opportunities to shape the record, if you're aware of the evidence rules relating to admissibility and relevance of documents, then you can do some good for your client in case the walls come tumbling down.

You can bring your sense of the document in court to bear on how you write the document and otherwise carry out the work.

Talk to the Litigators

Speaking of our friends in litigation (who just told us to work through contract language), let's note one other thing they often tell us.

Litigators say we should assume everything we do in writing — e-mails (whether internal or external), drafts, texts, communications with the other counsel — will eventually be produced in discovery or at least reviewed by lawyers, sometimes years later, working on a dispute or regulatory investigation.

So think about what you write down, consider those future readers, and, always, always maintain a professional and reasonable tone.

Snarkiness is tempting in the moment, generally fun, and always dumb.

You might also want to get to know the litigators down the hall.

Litigators and corporate lawyers, curiously, don't seem to interact nearly as much as one might expect. But even a short conversation with a seasoned litigator about a contract provision, or having her as a discussion partner when you're developing a piece of advice, can be enormously helpful. (This is yet another case where use of a visual can help you quickly brief a busy individual about a problem.)

Litigators have a stance toward the world that's different from ours, an awareness of evidence and dispute dynamics that can be striking, and we can really learn from those folks.

Protecting Privilege

Attorney-client privilege is another evidence doctrine that isn't just the concern of the litigators. You remember the rules: the privilege applies to a communication between an attorney and a client made in confidence for the purpose of seeking or obtaining legal advice.

For us, though, while privilege is there, it's generally not a top-of-mind issue. The odds that you'll work on a transaction that ends in litigation and generates a privilege dispute involving a specific communication between the client and you probably aren't super high.

Moreover, you'll find yourself in situations with your client and a group of other folks in the room (investment bankers, auditors, consultants, lower-level staff) whose presence may not be consistent with "confidential" communication. You're having a discussion in which legal advice is sought and given in the free flow of the meeting. The dynamics are such that you're

not going to kick out those folks to ensure confidentiality; indeed, hearing their point of view can enrich the discussion and improve the advice.

You may also see disparate practices in how firms and individual lawyers label documents and e-mail as "privileged and confidential" or "attorney-client communication."

So does that mean you can blow off privilege concerns and just go about your business?

No.

We need to pay attention. In some advisory situations we need to pay extra-special attention. In some transactional settings we need to be careful about how we handle information sharing. In some governance situations we need to shape the record appropriately. And in all situations we need to avoid the careless mistake.

Some suggestions:

Even though we live in an e-mail and texting world, think about whether it's best in some cases to talk with, rather than write to, the client. (Partners sometimes note that they would like junior attorneys to more often simply pick up the phone and call the client.)

It may be wise to educate clients about not automatically forwarding your e-mail, memo or report to others, and that sending stuff to you doesn't automatically make it privileged.

It's good to be aware of who's participating in a meeting or conference call, and to ask folks to step out as appropriate, as awkward as that may be.

In sensitive cases, you may want to encourage the client to note explicitly in its communication to you that the client is requesting legal advice. And, you may want to state in your communication back that you are responding to their request for legal advice.

This is obvious, but, be super-careful in e-mails about sending to the correct recipient, not using "reply all" unless you know who all is, and attaching the correct attachment. It's very easy to mess up here.

If you do mess up and inadvertently expose information, don't wait to fix it. Notify the recipient immediately that the e-mail or document contains privileged information and demand that they delete and make no use of it. (If this happens during litigation, you can act under Rule 26 of the Federal Rules of Civil Procedure or comparable state law.) If the recipient ignores you, follow up.

Your firm may have its own practice, and such marking is not dispositive, but it may be appropriate to mark only sensitive (not all) communications as "confidential," "attorney-client communication," "privileged and confidential," and the like.

If you're at a board or other meeting, and if feasible under the circumstances, try to plainly call out the "legal" advice in your remarks, and to excuse third parties from that portion of the discussion.

If you're doing the minutes for a board meeting, be sure to note the participation of counsel and the departure of third parties, and to not disclose the substance of the legal advice.

If you're doing a non-disclosure agreement for an acquisition or other transaction and privileged information may be shared, talk with your colleagues about a section addressing that topic specifically, and about accepted procedures for sharing such information. There are cases holding that parties to a transaction may be able to available themselves of a "common interest privilege," which permits parties aligned in interest with respect to litigation or regulatory matters to share

attorney-client communications without blowing the privilege.

You may also want to take a look at the several cases involving who (seller or buyer) holds the privilege with respect to pre-sale communications.

And, always remember that you have a serious duty under the professional responsibility rules to protect client confidences. That's entirely separate from, and broader than, the privilege rules.

There may be a 1% probability of a dispute where the status of a communication as privileged will be contested, but there is a 100% probability that the duty of confidentiality applies to you.

No excuses here: keep that confidential information under your hat.

Documents are One Part of the Story

Contracts and other documents, and the legal rules and processes (such as litigation) attendant to them, are not the only factors affecting how parties structure and manage their relationships.

As you likely talked about in Contracts, scholars have shown the centrality of industry norms, reputation, prospects of future business, and other non-legal influences in securing performance and resolving disputes.

Handshakes, the way things are done, future sales, and other dimensions of the relationship are really important. Businesses blend formal and informal mechanisms in defining, carrying out, and ending their work together.

These examinations of contracting behavior are instructive. Documents say what they say, and folks may have invested a lot of time and money in them, and they may look fancy and formal, and people may consult them, and angry people may litigate them, but documents aren't necessarily always the only word, or the last one.

Understanding that there are multiple factors at work in a given situation is really important for those of us who make and interpret documents for a living. (In-house lawyers come quickly to that recognition after spending some time inside a business.)

None of that diminishes the importance of getting the substance right, creating great documents, paying attention to document admissibility and use in litigation, and taking steps to protect privilege.

Our job is to execute crisply across all aspects of the work including positioning the client for judicial resolution of a problem.

But it does teach us, once again, to always pay attention to the broader business context and relationship and about the trust built (or not) in the course of the relationship. It also imparts a deeper understanding of, and a due sense of humility about, our role in helping a business get from state A to state B.

See You in Court

Thinking about litigation awareness gives us a nice opportunity to reflect on corporate lawyer work.

We can help position our client for litigation by listening to the client closely, doing great technical legal work, designing thoughtful decision-making processes, testing document content by working through scenarios, taking advantage of product functionality by incorporating favorable interpretation, dispute resolution, and remedial provisions (and generally paying attention to the boilerplate), creating a good record, being mindful of the evidence rules (including those relating to presumptions and admissions), assuming whatever we write will be read (in an unhappy context), learning from the litigators next door, and paying due attention to privilege.

In short, we think about the business, we imagine the future, we think about potential readers, we take advantage of what our products can do, and we're careful in our communications.

Litigation anticipation sounds like a job description for a corporate lawyer. We do our job right, and we do right by the client.

Final Thoughts: Being Mindful of Litigation

- Get the legal stuff right
- Take advantage of document functionality
- Take advantage of opportunities to shape the record
- Be mindful of privilege considerations
- Avoid the careless mistake
- Talk to the litigators now and then

9 / Why You Should Read SEC Filings

Lawyers regularly encounter (and you can learn a lot from reading) disclosure documents filed by companies with the SEC. This chapter introduces these useful materials.

Whether you have a corporate or commercial practice, you're going to run into filings by public companies with the Securities and Exchange Commission.

If you do corporate work, you study them when doing diligence for an acquisition or financing. You factor them into your deal plan. You draft them when you help a company sell stock or execute a merger where stock is the consideration. You review them as part of an ongoing advisory relationship.

If you do commercial work, you may study a counterparty's filings when working on a supply or licensing deal, or you may be asked to review portions of a draft filing describing a technology or regulatory regime.

Even if you don't regularly deal with public companies, SEC filings are still worth knowing about. You can learn a lot about business and financial reporting by reading them, and lawyers should always be learning about those subjects. From a career point of view, business and sector knowledge are good things if you imagine yourself going in-house at some point.

So it makes sense to know a little about what's in the core disclosure documents, and where they come from. That's what we'll cover here.

What's in these Documents: Business

SEC disclosures are full of facts. It's non-fiction, or at least it better be non-fiction.

Core filings contain extensive disclosure about the company itself. A filing may address business strategy, products, marketing, competition, customers, suppliers, technology, intellectual property, facilities, regulatory setting, and litigation. There is a section called "risk factors," a comprehensive review of risks associated with the industry, company, and ownership of the company's securities.

These documents also include lots of information about principal stockholders, directors, management, stock performance, executive compensation, related party transactions, and, as we saw, corporate governance arrangements and practices.

You can see that much of this disclosure is about a company's constituent relationships. You can also easily understand why in-house lawyers devote considerable time to study of competitors' filings; they can learn about what those companies are doing, and how they see the market.

If the filing relates to a securities offering, merger or other transaction, the document will contain extensive information about the background, rationale, terms, and consequences of the deal.

Filings often "incorporate by reference" information from prior filings. That's a common sense way of avoiding duplication and reducing the length of what can be pretty lengthy documents.

And a great thing (from a business lawyer's point of view): the rules require companies to submit key documents as exhibits to their filings. These include "material contracts," which can encompass all sorts of things, from leases to licenses to employment agreements.

The exhibits requirement means you can get rapid access to interesting and relevant documents, including the latest and greatest acquisition and financing agreements. Exhibits are a terrific source of marketplace precedent.

You will see that some filings include certifications signed by the CEO and CFO regarding the accuracy and completeness of the disclosures, compliance with applicable rules, and company disclosure and accounting processes.

The certification regime is a little like the officers' certificates delivered at a transaction closing; having big shots sign first-person statements does tend to concentrate the corporate mind on getting things right.

Happily, the SEC requires disclosure documents to be written in plain language, with bullets and tables and the like. Hurrah!

There's a lot of business information in SEC filings.

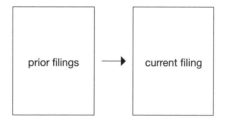

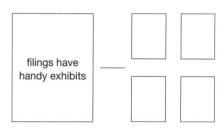

Filings are full of facts about the business: strategy, products, customers, risks, properties, management, and on and on.

If the filing relates to a merger, securities offering, or other transaction, it will include lots of information about the deal.

Filings may "incorporate by reference" prior filings. Which is another reason we better get it right the first time around.

Filings often include "material contracts" and other documents as exhibits. That's a great way to find marketplace precedents. (And another way lawyer work becomes visible.)

What's in these Documents: Financial

SEC documents are full of numbers and discussions of numbers. There's a ton of useful information here.

The rules require inclusion of financial statements prepared in accordance with generally accepted accounting rules (GAAP) and SEC requirements. You've no doubt heard that lawyers should be familiar with accounting and financial statements. That is absolutely true. SEC filings, which contain both full statements with extensive notes and separate summary presentations, are great vehicles for building your knowledge and confidence in this area.

One help: the rules require commentary about the financial results. For example, core filings include something called "Management's Discussion and Analysis of Financial Condition

and Results of Operations," known as MD&A. It's simply a narrative walk-through of the numbers. The MD&A typically describes the key components of revenues and expenses, and marches right down the income statement, explaining changes in specific line items from the prior comparable fiscal period (e.g., third quarter of last year) to the current period (this year's Q3).

The MD&A also covers "liquidity and capital resources." Liquidity means access to cash, and cash is king, so cash availability and future demands on cash are of considerable interest. The discussion includes disclosure about principal sources of cash (including cash on hand and access to credit), and a table showing certain commitments, such as debt obligations, that consume major cash.

Another help: the MD&A and financial statements describe significant accounting policies. For example, a filing may explain how and when the company recognizes revenue from a sale or other event. That's important, because it helps you both understand the numbers and better compare the results of company X to company Y. The policies covered necessarily depend on the nature of the business; inventory valuation, for example, is not a big issue for a social media company — but it certainly is for a clothing retailer.

Companies sometimes supplement their reported results with "non-GAAP" measures that they believe more accurately (or least positively) reflect their results or that are commonly used by investors to gauge performance. These measures include or exclude amounts from the most directly comparable GAAP measure. You'll run into items such as "EBITDA" and "free cash flow," common measures of earning power and cash generation. The SEC requires companies to define and explain why they use such items and to reconcile them to the most comparable GAAP measures.

And companies may report other quantitative data not required or encompassed by the accounting rules, such as information about operations. The social media company, for example, may report daily active users, mobile users, and similar items. The clothing retailer may disclose store openings, closures, and sales per square foot.

If the filing relates to a transaction, then the document may contain "pro forma" statements. These are simply financial statements adjusted to reflect the impact of the deal. In a stock offering, for example, the pro forma balance sheet will show the cash infusion from the offering and the resulting capital structure. This kind of information is useful for folks deciding whether to buy shares in the deal; they can see the post-offering balance sheet and financial position of the company.

Finally, filings include not only numbers but also disclosure and assurances about the processes used in developing and reporting the numbers. The rules require statements by management about "disclosure controls," the company's procedures for ensuring disclosure-relevant information is communicated to management on a timely basis, and "internal controls," the processes designed to ensure the reliability of financial reporting and proper preparation of the financial statements.

So there can be a lot of learning in SEC filings — about the sector, about the company, about accounting principles, about how companies define the market and measure their performance, and about the latest transaction structures and terms.

You can also learn a lot of business, accounting, and financial vocabulary, which is always a good thing.

Where They Come From: Issuing Securities

One place these documents come from is a company selling stock or other securities.

The basic idea, of course, is that investors need information in making investment decisions. The Securities Act of 1933 accordingly requires "issuers" of securities to provide information to investors and sets out rules for how the issuer conducts the offering.

Companies issue stock in different ways. They may sell shares to investors in a public offering. They may issue stock to employees as compensation. They may use stock as the consideration in a merger. They may sell shares to a business partner as part of a larger commercial collaboration. Or a smaller company may issue shares through an equity crowdfunding platform.

In some cases, such as an initial public offering, issuers must "register" the shares under the Securities Act. They file with the SEC a lengthy document called a "registration statement." The registration statement contains a "prospectus," which is the principal disclosure document.

In an IPO and sometimes in other settings, the SEC reviews the filing and comes back with comments. The company and agency then work through rounds of revision and explanation until the SEC declares the filing "effective" and clears the company to sell the securities.

There are "forms" under the Securities Act that specify the required disclosures for different types of offerings. For example, an issuer uses Form S-1 for an IPO, S-4 for an issuance in a merger or other business combination, and S-8 for an issuance of securities through employee stock option and other equity compensation plans. The extent of required disclosure is a function of entity size, reporting history, type of transaction, and other factors.

Not every issuance must be registered with the SEC. Certain securities and certain transactions are exempt from registration. Examples include smaller offerings and "private placements" to institutional investors. These are quite common; you'll run into them in Silicon Valley, on Wall Street, and on Main Street. A fair chunk of corporate finance work involves these sorts of deals.

So: if you come across a registration statement or a prospectus, a company is selling securities.

The Securities Act covers issuances of securities.

EVENT	IPO	Employee stock	Subsequent bond issuance	Merger
	↓	↓	↓	↓
FORM	S-1	S-8	S-3	S-4

Securities are issued in multiple ways

· Private offerings
· Initial public offerings
· Mergers
· Employee equity compensation
· Strategic alliances

Key issues

· Exemptions from registration
· Form choice and
  required disclosure
· Conduct of offering

Securities Act forms specify required disclosures for securities offerings

· Different forms for different transaction types
· Registration statement includes prospectus and exhibits
· Extent of disclosure a function of entity size, reporting history, type of transaction, and other factors

How IPOs Work

Speaking of IPOs: here's how they work.

The company going public hires a group of investment banks to "underwrite" the offering. The bankers do two main things.

First, they help draft the prospectus and shape the strategy for marketing the offering to investors.

Second, they line up purchasers for the shares. These buyers may include big institutional investors, such as mutual funds, as well as retail (regular people) investors.

The prospectus drafting process is time consuming. It's not easy to tell a company's story in a persuasive and compelling but accurate and substantiated way. There are multiple people engaged in day-long "drafting sessions," all with a point of view. This is group writing at its extreme.

What's more, the banks have liability under the securities laws for the disclosures in the prospectus. They can defend against such claims if they establish a "due diligence" defense under the statute. That means the banks, with their lawyers, ask a lot of questions and review a lot of documents along the way.

When it comes time to launch the deal, the company and the banks agree on a price at which the banks will sell the shares to investors. The company then sells the shares to the banks at a discount to the public price, and the banks sell to the public at the public price. That "underwriting discount" is how the banks make their money on the deal.

These arrangements are documented through a contract called an "underwriting" or "purchase" agreement. As you would expect, these documents contain extensive representations by the company, covenants by the company relating to the offering process, and complex indemnification provisions in favor of the underwriters.

(Underwriting agreements are a nice demonstration of contract functionality. The reps, for example, are a diligence tool. The lawyers who advise investment banks know how to take advantage of contract functionality.)

Quite a number of other things go on in an IPO as well. The company needs to choose a stock exchange. Company executives and the banks do "road show" meetings with prospective investors. Individual stockholders may sell shares in the offering in addition to those sold by the company. Company insiders and key stockholders may sign "lock-up agreements" where they agree not to sell any shares for X days after the offering, in order not to depress the price.

As in any transaction: planning, project management, people, and paper.

Investment banks help the company tell its story and find investors.

CORPORATION

Sells shares
at $30/share

Investment Banks

Sell shares at
$35/share

Investors

The banks do extensive
diligence, help write the
prospectus, and line
up investors.

This is how
the banks
make money
on the deal.

Where They Come From: Public Companies

The second place disclosure documents come from is a company that is publicly held as a result of an IPO or otherwise has a bunch of stockholders. These companies are subject to the Securities Exchange Act of 1934.

The Exchange Act contemplates three core types of disclosures by companies: filings to be made on a *periodic* basis, in connection with *recurring events*, and in connection with certain *non-recurring developments*. The Exchange Act, like the Securities Act, has different forms for different types of filings.

Public companies are required to make (periodic) filings on an annual and on a quarterly basis.

The annual report (Form 10-K) is a whopper. It contains audited financial statements and detailed disclosure about a variety of business, risk, financial performance, management, controls, and other topics.

The quarterly report (Form 10-Q) is filed after each of the first three quarters. It contains unaudited quarterly statements and more limited disclosure about results, with a focus on key changes in financial condition from the end of the preceding fiscal year, and changes in results from the comparable period in the prior year.

Periodic disclosure requirements, as we saw, can be important factors in developing a deal or product release calendar.

Public companies must provide stockholders with a proxy statement in connection with the (recurring) annual stockholders' meeting. The proxy contains extensive information about directors and executives, governance, and executive compensation (all useful to know before a vote for directors), as well as about matters to be considered and voted on at the meeting. Public companies must also distribute proxy statements in connection with special stockholders' meetings, including those relating to merger approvals.

Finally, public companies must disclose, on Form 8-K, specified (non-recurring) events promptly after they occur. These events include entry into material agreements, departure or election of directors, and completion of material acquisitions or dispositions of assets.

When you're planning a deal, or when something big happens, legal and finance folks will be thinking about Exchange Act requirements and deadlines.

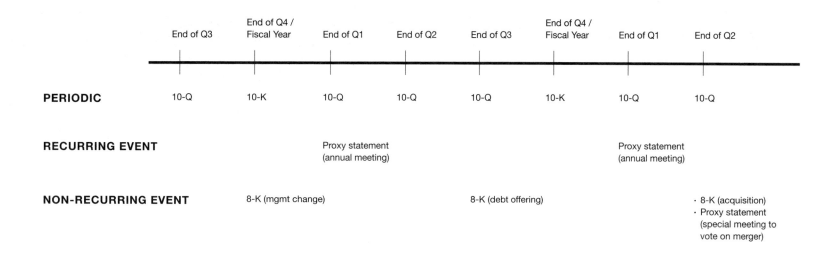

ANNUAL / FORM 10-K

· Contains audited financial statements, MD&A, and disclosure about business, risk factors, management, and stockholders

· Includes internal controls and disclosure controls reports

· Includes exhibits such as material contracts

· Certified by CEO and CFO

· Must be filed within specified period after end of fiscal year

QUARTERLY / FORM 10-Q

· Contains unaudited interim period statements, MD&A, disclosure about performance during quarter, and updated risk factors

· Includes relevant exhibits

· Certified by CEO and CFO

· Must be filed within specified period after end of quarter

CURRENT / FORM 8-K

· Vehicle for real time disclosure of specified events

· Events include entry into or termination of material agreement; departure or election of directors or principal officers; completion of acquisition or disposition of assets; modifications to rights of security holders; change in auditor

· Includes relevant exhibits

· Not certified by CEO and CFO

· Generally, must be filed within four business days of triggering event

PROXY / SCHEDULE 14A

· Distributed in connection with annual or other stockholder meeting involving voting

· Contains extensive information about management, corporate governance, and executive compensation

Regulation S-K

There is good news about these filings: the basic source of disclosure requirements under both statutes is the same.

A big set of rules called Regulation S-K sets out required disclosures for registration statements under the Securities Act and for periodic and other filings under the Exchange Act.

Reg S-K is long and detailed, but the basic mechanics are straightforward.

You figure out what form you need to prepare. As we saw, there are different Securities Act forms depending on the nature of the transaction and the issuer, and there are different Exchange Act forms for different reporting periods and triggers.

The form will contain a series of "items." These items will say things like "Furnish the information required by Item 102 of Regulation S-K."

You look at Item 102 of Reg S-K.

You draft the disclosure in line with the requirements set out in Item 102.

That's it.

Familiarity with the key forms and with Reg S-K will enable you to navigate SEC filings much more quickly. It's like learning the typical organizational scheme of a credit or acquisition agreement.

Learning the vocab is useful, too; in the office you'll hear lots of shorthand references ("do we have to 8-K that?" "is that a 404 item?"), and it's good to know what folks are talking about.

Regulation S-K details the disclosure
requirements for both Securities Act
and Exchange Act filings.

FORM   **ITEM IN FORM**   **REG S-K ITEM**   **DISCLOSURE**

Determine what form to prepare.

Items in form will point you to items in Reg S-K.

Study relevant Reg S-K item.

Draft the disclosure as required by Reg S-K item.

Working on these Documents

If you do securities or capital markets work, you may start out by doing "form checks" or "rule checks," where you take a draft fling and confirm that the disclosures are fully responsive to form and S-K requirements. You will sit with the rules on one side of your desk or computer screen and the draft disclosure on the other, and go back and forth, with attention to both substance and presentation. It requires discipline and focus.

And, if you write these things, you've got a lot of work to do.

You need to review prior period filings, gather relevant documents, talk to the client, take a look at competitors' filings, examine prior client public communications (consistency is obviously important), find out if the SEC has provided guidance about particular rules, document your homework, and draft the disclosure.

This is tough duty. You have to deal with the extensive content rules. There's all that business homework and substantiation to get done. There's the writing, which is almost entirely about business, and which needs to reflect your study, the content rules, the format and style rules, the collaboration with and accommodation of multiple contributors, and the unbending filing deadlines.

And you have to do all this with an eye toward multiple potential readers, and with a keen awareness of legal liability.

If you're in-house or otherwise responsible for the filing, there's also considerable project management involved.

You need to coordinate internal activity at the company, leave time for senior management, auditor, and possibly board or board committee review, make sure the work is done to back up the CEO and CFO certifications, gather needed exhibits, chase down signatures, and ensure data and messaging consistency across the filing and any related press releases, scripts for earnings calls with analysts, and talking points for employee communications and media inquiries. (Recall all those constituents.)

This blend of business study, group writing, attention to detail, and project management is starting to sound familiar, huh?

Learn Your Way Around

SEC filings are useful to know about even if you don't do securities work. You can learn about business and financial reporting by reading them. That in and of itself makes them useful tools for career-long students of business: the more you know, the better you can listen, and the better you can observe, advise, and plan.

Moreover, having a sense of the required disclosures, the reporting calendar, and the work required to prepare these documents, is valuable no matter the nature of your practice. You'll be more familiar with the resource demands on your client, you'll know where to look for information, and you'll bring useful data to the table when planning a deal or preparing to launch a product or corporate initiative.

So: gather up your clients' (and key competitors') 10-Ks, find yourself a good glossary of accounting and financial terms, and dig in.

It's worth the effort.

Final Thoughts: Why You Should Read SEC Filings

- Know the basic disclosure scheme

- Be familiar with the core forms

- Take a look at Reg S-K

- Read some filings (especially your clients')

10 / Doing Pro Bono

Corporate lawyers can do great pro bono work. This chapter is about working with nonprofit organizations, the typical client in a corporate pro bono engagement.

People sometimes think pro bono is mostly for litigators. A lawyer represents an individual in a small case, or helps a public interest firm with a big case.

As it turns out, though, corporate lawyers do pro bono, too, and of course pro bono is a professional responsibility of all lawyers. Our projects often involve representation of nonprofit organizations; indeed, the Model Rules of Professional Conduct call on us to provide free or reduced-fee services to charitable, educational, and similar organizations.

So it makes sense to spend a little time learning about a common type of nonprofit, the charitable organization, in case you're among the many who didn't encounter nonprofit law in law school.

As we'll see, pro bono work involves a neat combination of familiar and new legal contexts. It can be both intellectually engaging and personally gratifying on multiple levels. And your work can be enormously helpful to an organization in a variety of ways.

Think: corporate lawyer as community resource.

It's a Corporation...

The first thing to know is that much is familiar.

Charities are typically organized as nonprofit corporations under state corporation law. Let's say that again: they are corporations.

So, from a corporate perspective, they have the same perpetual life and limited liability attributes of their business counterparts. They can have subsidiaries and affiliates. They can do mergers. They have financial statements. They have boards of directors, board committees, and officers. Directors have duties of care and loyalty.

From a commercial perspective, nonprofits have physical facilities and contractual relationships. They run programs. They rent, lease, and share real property. They create and license intellectual property and build brands. They borrow money. They deal with program and geographic expansion. They have employees and benefit plans. They have tort exposures.

This sounds familiar. There is a lot of good solid governance, contract, real estate, intellectual property, and other legal work here.

These corporate and commercial
attributes look pretty familiar.

CORPORATE

- Perpetual life
- Limited liability
- Subsidiaries
- Affiliates
- Mergers
- Boards of directors

COMMERCIAL

- Real estate
- Contractual relationships
- Programs
- Intellectual property
- Brands
- Employees

...But There are Some Differences

There are, though, some rather important differences between business corporations and nonprofit charitable corporations.

For one thing, a nonprofit doesn't have any stockholders. Nobody owns a nonprofit. There's no equity. It doesn't pay dividends. Some charities have "members" that elect directors, but in most cases the directors elect their successors.

Second, unlike businesses, nonprofits are limited in their activities. Businesses can largely do what they want, but charities must engage in, and operate exclusively for, charitable purposes. That's required under state nonprofit law and it's spelled out in the organization's articles of incorporation. Its assets, by law, are irrevocably dedicated to charitable purposes.

That doesn't mean charities can't make money or run businesses — after all, they have to keep the doors open — but it does mean that they are focused on, and must be focused on, activities that further their stated mission.

Third, charities typically are exempt from federal and state income taxes. There are some exceptions, but generally revenue is tax free to the organization. And donors to the charity may take a deduction for their contributions.

As you might expect, the IRS has extensive rules about what it takes to obtain and keep tax-exempt status. The first and foremost rule requires the charity to be organized and operated exclusively for charitable purposes. (The IRS refers to those as the "organizational" and "operational" tests.) Other rules concern political activity, such as lobbying and

advocating for candidates, and, as we'll see, insider behavior and external disclosure.

Fourth, the IRS and the state attorney general are the principal regulators of charities. The IRS monitors organizational adherence to the requirements for tax exemption and can levy taxes or even revoke exempt status if a charity fails to comply. State attorneys general have broad oversight authority. They can examine actions by the charity's board, use of funds by the organization, fundraising activities, proposed mergers, and other matters.

There's one other big difference: people give money to charities. Most folks don't just give money to businesses. We better take a look at charitable revenue.

There are some big differences between
business and nonprofit corporations.

- No stockholders
- No dividends
- Assets dedicated to charitable purposes
- No income tax
- Limits on political activity
- IRS and state attorney general are regulators
- People donate to charities

Money Sources

When you think of charitable revenues, you think of donations from individuals. You might also think of grants from philanthropic foundations such as the Gates Foundation.

But there's more than gifts and grants.

Governments pay nonprofits to perform services. A lot of social services are funded this way.

Charities charge for products and services; think about buying items at a Goodwill store or paying tuition at your local law school or admission at your favorite art museum. (The IRS calls this "program service revenue" or "exempt function revenue.")

Nonprofits rent out facilities for events and license their brands. Companies pay them to sponsor events. Charities fortunate enough to have endowments earn income on their investments.

Check out the income statement for a charity and compare it with that of a business. The statement for the latter may simply have a "Net sales" line at the top. The statement for the charity may well have multiple line items: donations, foundation grants, government grants, services, special events, investment income.

Charities spend an enormous amount of time raising money and managing these various funding sources. (There is legal work associated with these various revenue streams, too.) And, remember, charities don't have the ability to sell stock and raise equity capital; they're always on the lookout for new money.

Charities spend a lot of time
raising money and managing
multiple funding sources.

· Individual donations
· Government grants
· Government contracts
· Foundation grants
· Product and service sales
· Royalties
· Corporate sponsorships
· Endowment income

$$$

Money Uses

If you gave money to a charity and then the charity spent it all on something entirely unrelated to its mission, you'd probably be upset, right? What if the charity used it on a sweetheart deal for the chief executive?

And, do you think the IRS might be unhappy if an outfit not paying taxes behaved that way? How about the attorney general? Doesn't that kind of behavior by a charity just seem wrong?

That suggests a central theme of nonprofit law: charitable dollars are to be used for charitable purposes. Charitable money is for public, not private, purposes.

Charities, needless to say, must use their funds in line with their stated charitable mission. Remember, their activities are limited by their articles, their assets by law are dedicated to charitable purposes, and their tax exemption depends on operating in furtherance of their stated purpose.

Moreover, there can be serious trouble under both state and federal law if insiders like directors or senior executives engage in self-dealing or the charity provides undue benefit to them. (The IRS calls this "private inurement.") There can be personal exposure for individual board members, and in some cases the entity may even lose its tax-exemption.

Nonprofits better not make fraudulent statements in their fundraising solicitations about how they'll use the money, either.

Charities also have to be careful in their contractual relationships with third parties to be sure the arrangement advances the charitable purpose of the entity and not the private interest of the other party. (The IRS calls that "private benefit.").

There are laws relating to specific interactions between charities and private businesses. For example, state statutes address "commercial co-venturer" and fundraising arrangements with businesses, and the IRS pays close attention to joint ventures between charities and taxable entities. (This is another example of how the identity of the actors in a particular situation tells us a lot about potential legal concerns.)

You'll see these concerns at work in governance practices, disclosure requirements, collaboration design, and elsewhere. Use of charitable money is a big deal, and use of charitable money by those in positions of influence over a charity is an especially big deal.

Charitable dollars are for charitable purposes.

Money with Strings Attached

There's another interesting feature of charitable revenue.

Donors can put restrictions on how the money is used. They can put strings on it. Those strings are binding on the charity.

You see this when you walk around a university campus; there's the Redd Family Center for the Study of Mars or the like. Every now and then you hear about a case where a donor's family sues a college or a museum about its alleged failure to use the donation in accordance with the terms of great-grandmother's gift.

(For those who are doctrinally-minded, there can be some sticky legal issues concerning things like standing to sue for violations of gift restrictions, or the treatment of restricted funds in a bankruptcy case.)

Grants from foundations generally work that way, too; the philanthropy is funding a particular initiative or program. That restriction is written right into the contract. For a charity, the money is great, but it also requires the organization to track its use closely and then report on its use. A charity also needs to resist the temptation to accept a gift if the gift would require it to stray from its priorities or strain its capacity.

Compare that restricted funds notion to when you buy groceries. You don't tell Whole Foods that they can use your money solely for the purpose of building a new deli, right?

Donors can put restrictions on
how their money is used.

Restriction on use

Reporting and Disclosure

Let's finish with a quick look at financial reporting and disclosure.

Charities, like businesses, prepare balance sheets (called a "statement of financial position"), income statements ("statement of activities"), and statements of cash flow (same name). They also prepare a fourth statement called the "statement of functional expenses." This provides a detailed breakdown, by key program, of how the charity spends its money.

The statement of activities presents expense information in three broad categories: program, management and general, and fundraising expenses.

That convention, together with the requirement for a statement of functional expenses, reflects a familiar principle: charitable dollars should be use for charitable purposes.

Donors and nonprofit watchdogs really want to see how the money is used; among other things,

they're interested in the percentage of funds spent on programs versus overhead.

There's a second unique feature of nonprofit financial statements.

Recall that donors can place restrictions on use of donated funds. These contractual limits are reflected in the statements; if you see "restricted assets," you'll know what's going on. Users of the financials need that information in order to assess the financial flexibility of the organization.

(This is another example of a contract term having an accounting effect, one of those "impacts" we look for when we read contracts as lawyers.)

And of course nonprofit financials don't have a stockholders' equity section on the balance sheet because nonprofits don't have stockholders. Instead, they report "net assets."

Finally, charities file information returns with the IRS on something called Form 990. This is the best tax return you'll ever read. It's full

of information about programs, governance, financial condition, executive compensation, financial reporting practices, related party transactions, revenue composition, and so on. It's not as complete or easy to follow as a 10-K, but it's still useful. And, unlike a business, charities must make their tax returns public; you can find them through the guidestar.org website.

You can learn a lot about a charity by looking at its financials and 990. Who would have thought a tax return could be so helpful?

You Can Do a Lot of Good

You can easily imagine how corporate lawyers can be useful to these organizations. Charities are corporations that deal with governance, contracts, intellectual property, tort, real estate, employment, and other matters.

You're well-positioned to help out. You might, for example, review and update a charity's bylaws and board committee charters. (It's an exercise similar to cleaning up a company before an IPO or sale.) You might help a charity think about a potential merger. You might create template contracts, or give advice about IP protection, or do a training session on board responsibilities.

There are challenges. Finding time in view of billable hour expectations is problematic; smaller and more discrete projects may be a good idea. Your firm may require a tax partner to oversee work for tax-exempt organizations, and those people are busy.

But it's worth your serious consideration for reasons in addition to meeting your professional obligations.

First, pro bono work can be intellectually engaging. We have to deal with the usual corporate and commercial stuff. And then we have to look through the nonprofit lens: fidelity to mission, proper use of charitable funds, and so on. We need to consider additional legal rules and reputational concerns, and to think about how to structure and document the deal or activity within the charitable framework.

In short, we have to put on more layers. It's the same drill we've seen before: look, label, figure out what to do, build the product. The legal knowledge, analytical skills, and document disciplines you have, the visual and other tools you deploy along the way... all are directly relevant.

Second, pro bono engagements may result in your having a larger role than you typically would on a project for a commercial client. You, not the partner or senior associate, are doing the docs, client counseling, and board presentation.

Third, if a project through the firm is hard to put together, consider joining the board of a charity. Your work as a director will not only benefit the charity but also, through your exposure to organizational realities and oversight responsibilities, nicely inform the advice you give to your law firm clients. Just be sure to follow whatever guidelines your firm may have about such service, and be mindful of which hat you're wearing (director or lawyer) when you're at board meetings and the like.

Fourth, nonprofits tend to be deeply and openly appreciative of pro bono support and board service. They are grateful for your help, and they say so, with a smile. You feel that, and it feels good.

Fifth, and maybe most importantly, you're doing the work in the context of helping someone who helps other people.

Can't beat that.

Final Thoughts: Doing Pro Bono

- Read the 990 and financials
- Know that mission is all
- Know that charitable dollars are for charitable purposes
- Think about structure and language given the legal framework
- Consider joining the board of a nonprofit

11 / Helping Your Client

Clients have tough jobs. This chapter offers some observations and practical suggestions for working effectively with your clients.

The client representatives you work with have really difficult jobs.

Think about the lives of corporate executives.

They deal with (and worry about) all sorts of things. They are accountable for business results, corporate reputation, transaction success, stock price, employee development, you name it.

Their decisions and behaviors are under constant scrutiny, internally and externally.

Their work is visible; businesses relentlessly measure and report financial and operational performance. Stock prices move, investors respond, social media explodes, careers soar and crash.

General counsels have gigantic jobs, too.

This chapter explores some way we can, in our everyday work, serve and support our clients, and make their lives at least a little bit easier.

Executive and GC Life

The corner office is an intense place.

Executives make decisions all the time, one after the other, both material and mundane. They are bombarded by information, demands, criticisms, and requests.

Think back to that map showing the constituents of a corporation. Imagine a person, not an abstract legal entity, at the middle of that map. There's a lot coming at that individual with the big job.

Internally, employees pay deep attention to senior management, to what they say and to the tone they set. Executives are always on.

They're also wildly busy. Their schedules are packed. They are pressed and have a lot on their minds. In many ways, executives have less control over their schedules than do others in the company; if a board member, major customer, or regulator calls, they jump. They don't get a lot of quiet time, especially now that airplanes are Wi-Fi equipped.

The job of the general counsel isn't exactly a stroll in the park, either.

GCs are typically members of the senior management team and, as such, have substantial leadership roles. They are responsible for the legal affairs of the corporation, from managing litigation to protecting intellectual property to avoiding corruption overseas to staying on top of dozens of subsidiaries. The breadth of legal issues they face is enormous.

GCs lead a business unit (a non-revenue-generating unit, from the business perspective) and sometimes multiple business units. They are responsible for managing a budget and for motivating and developing their teams.

At a more personal level, general counsels report to the CEO (who can fire them) but have an independent relationship with the CEO's boss (the board). This is not always a comfortable position. They are employees, with the economic dependency that creates. Yet they have a professional obligation to provide independent and objective advice.

General counsels have one formal client (the corporation), but on the ground they and their teams have multiple clients across the business and around the world: product development, marketing, sales, finance, and other units, often running diverse businesses in multiple countries.

These are really, really tough jobs.

Your job is to help these folks. What can you do?

Regulators	Tax Authorities	Auditor	Stock Exchange	Analysts

Lenders	Bondholders

Stockholders

Suppliers	Alliance Partners	♀ EXECUTIVE	Customers	Consumers

Landlords	Licensors	Board	Competitors	Licensees

Employees

Contractors	Unions

Media	NGOs	Public

How You Can Help

There's a lot you can do.

You know the business. What it sells, how it sells, principal constituents, key metrics, internal calendar, and so on. You study the financials, review the 10-K, look at the website, read the media coverage, use the product or service.

Business knowledge deepens your ability to listen, see, think, and advise.

You listen closely and ask (well-informed) questions. Clients sometime say the best thing a lawyer does for them is to serve as a discussion partner. That's right in line with our professional obligation to provide independent judgment and candid advice.

If you're giving advice, you understand that business situations, from an executive's viewpoint, require consideration of multiple and often competing constituencies, objectives and timeframes, with legal being but one among them.

To that end, you're not afraid to offer business as well as legal advice. Clients welcome an objective assessment from a smart individual who regularly advises other companies; they want your point of view.

You plan well, get the advice right, deliver it confidently and not arrogantly, and execute the project with a minimum of drama. The executive has enough sources of heartburn in her life; she doesn't need you to give her more.

You understand management time is precious. You have a plan for phone calls and meetings with clients. You make efficient and effective use of their time.

If you're working on a deal, you understand that the executive is focused on getting the deal done; she has an objective, transaction completion is a step in her achieving that objective, and she wants to get back to running her business. For you, the deal is your life; for her, well, she has a day job.

You understand that the client likely won't be all that interested in the technical details or the ups and downs of the daily struggle; she will trust you to know your stuff and to deal with the bumps. As such, you craft your communications accordingly.

You are thoughtful about implementation realities: compliance, reporting, administration, coordination. You make the extra effort to take them into account in your advice, document review, negotiations, deliverable design, and communications.

You tailor standard documents to client specifics, and think about practical training and guidance tools for client staff. In-house lawyers (likely your principal contacts) are often eager for materials to provide to their own clients across the business.

You understand that while big transactions like acquisitions may be a largely technical project for you, they can have huge career and personal consequences for the people you're dealing with, at both your client's company and on the other side of the table.

There are real human as well as commercial dimensions of deals. You reflect that in your dealings with individuals, including being patient, civil, and available at their convenience. Soft skills are really important in hard situations.

Lawyers who understand and respond to client realities are respected, valued, and viewed fondly by their clients.

Keep it Short

Another good thing: be brief. Get to the point.

Don't go past one page for cheat sheets, talking points, flow charts, or other implementation documents.

Keep e-mails and other communication documents short, crisp, and practical.

Use bullets and numbered lists whenever you can.

Be clear about any action needed from the client. What do you need them to do?

Be thoughtful about the content of e-mail subject lines; that's what the client sees on first glance at the smartphone.

Think about how attachments will appear when opened on a phone; consider sending redlines in a PDF, not a track changes, version.

Keep document filenames short and clear; the idea is to make it easy for the client to recognize and save.

Make sure the filenames of any attachments are consistent with the document nature and title.

Open attachments before sending, to be sure that they're the documents you want to send. And don't forget to actually attach the attachments.

Simple, obvious, and really important stuff — and routinely messed up by folks.

Again: think crazy-busy person reading on a phone (who is under stress).

These are ways you can carry out your professional duty of communication in a thoughtful, empathetic, and practical way.

Get to the point.

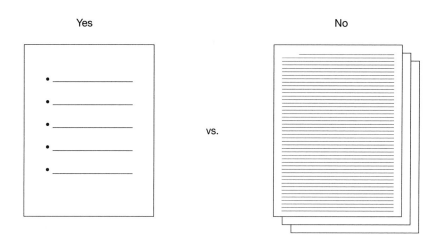

Yes   No

vs.

Make Life Easier

One angle for thinking about working with clients is to use the framework provided by the professional responsibility rules. Consider the duties not as obligations or behavioral floors but instead as values and ways of working.

We can read a lot into the duties of competence, diligence, and independent professional judgment: deep business understanding, close listening, sophisticated legal knowledge, thorough analysis, thoughtful advice, methodical deal management, careful document design and execution.

We can read a lot into our duty of communication: being mindful of reader realities, keeping our communications crisp and concise, being as practical as we can be.

Another way of thinking about client (and for that matter colleague) interactions — particularly in the early stages of your career when you're dealing with a lot of logistics — is the notion of "making life easier for the other person."

You make life easier for the client not only through getting the legal and communication stuff right but also in little ways.

Folks notice and appreciate the well-organized binder, or the well-planned meeting, or the plentiful lead time for providing information or signing documents.

You respect a client and her time that way.

Your colleagues are busy and pressured, too. As with clients, drama is to be avoided.

Reliability, productivity, responsiveness, preparation, and good cheer are welcomed. A sticky note on a draft, a stack of background documents on the chair, a document ready before it is requested, sufficient copies already made… those incidents of awareness, thoughtfulness, and courtesy can go a long way. And playing badly in the sandbox with your colleagues can go a long way in the wrong direction.

Making life easier is a useful if corny formulation for helping appreciate the many dimensions, large and small, of the outward focus and orientation of a corporate lawyer. Bedside manner matters in our profession, too.

You can do a lot to make life easier for clients and colleagues.

PROFESSIONAL DUTIES

· Competence
· Diligence
· Professional judgment
· Communication

PROFESSIONAL WORK

· Deep business understanding
· Deep legal knowledge
· Close listening and observation
· Thorough analysis
· Thoughtful and practical advice
· Disciplined project management
· Careful document execution
· Crisp communication

PROFESSIONAL WAYS OF WORKING

· Anticipation
· Organization
· Preparation
· Resourcefulness
· Attention to detail
· Responsiveness
· Reliability
· Thoughtfulness
· Courtesy

PROFESSIONAL OUTCOMES

· Well-served client
· Well-supported colleague

Final Thoughts: Helping Your Client

- Know the business
- Listen closely
- Keep it short
- Be thoughtful about e-mail, including attachments
- Make life easier, in all respects

Conclusion

Corporate lawyers develop advice, plan transactions, and build functional objects. We need to be methodical, disciplined, imaginative, thoughtful, and deeply attuned to our clients.

In advice development, we consider both relationships with constituents, such as the license of a trademark, and unilateral activity by our client, such as board meeting preparation or financial disclosure.

In constituent relationship matters, we identify actors, look at and characterize flows, and develop potential interventions. Interventions may be internal in nature (e.g., a refinement in a policy or practice) or external (a new disclosure, or a change in a contract). In internal matters, we're often focused on process design and information management.

Advisory work is interesting in that we have to break down complex situations so we can see what's going on. Then, with our imagination and technical knowledge, we start adding layers as we think about what we've found and how we can affect it in positive ways for the client.

Transaction planning combines advice development with project management.

We look at the flows that make up the transaction. We think about their implications. We figure out a structure that accommodates them. We consider the impact of a transaction on the actor's constituents, and about communications with those constituents. We identify who needs to approve the transaction, and develop the process for that approval. We determine what documents we need for these flows, communications, and approvals.

We capture all this in plans, timelines, and lists. And then we line up resources, manage the work like crazy, and execute on the ground; project management is a core feature of deal work.

Transactional work is interesting in that there can be lots of factors that influence deal structure and process; our job is to sort through everything, identify what needs to get done by when, and then make it happen.

In both advisory and deal settings, whether we have a corporate or a commercial practice, we encounter and produce documents of all kinds.

Legal documents are business documents; they're full of facts, processes, and numbers. Documents are highly functional. They do things out in the world. They have meaningful practical consequences. People use and rely upon them. Documents often relate to one another and sometimes conflict with one another.

Some documents are pretty long, dense, and intimidating.

Documents often, though, reflect common sense concerns. They have characteristic organizational schemes and conventions. There are ways for breaking them down when you read them, and there are ways to organize your thoughts when you're constructing them.

Thinking of legal document as products, and treating reading as a professional activity, are useful angles of approach to document work. By appreciating the characteristics of our products, and by reading for multiple purposes with imagination and discipline, we can evaluate documents more thoroughly and thoughtfully, and we can design and execute better products for our clients.

Document work is interesting given the fact that we need to be mindful not only of substance but also implications (litigation and otherwise), legal craft, and technical execution. We have

to pay attention to the big picture and the little picture. There's a lot to see and think about in these things.

Use of diagrams and other visuals is a terrific practical technique for folks who give advice, plan deals, and work with documents. Visuals mobilize knowledge, externalize thought, convey abstract concepts, promote faster processing, facilitate collaboration, permit application of layers (literally), prompt reinterpretation, and spark new ideas. Timelines and calendars, like diagrams and process maps, are similarly basic but effective and useful tools in this line of work.

And doing everything we can across all that we do to make our clients lives easier, from business understanding to nuanced analysis to crisp communication to bedside manner, is intellectually challenging, professionally responsible, and personally gratifying.

In practicing our craft we can do a lot of good for folks, and we can have good fun doing it.

In practicing our craft,
we can do a lot of good for our clients,
and have good fun doing it.

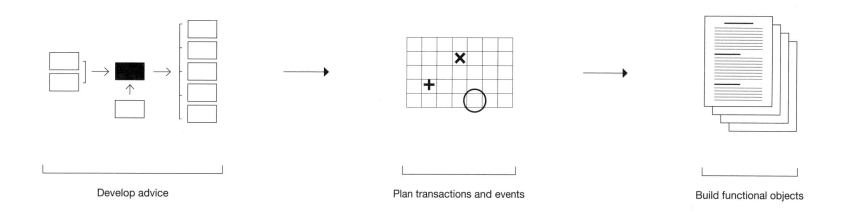

Develop advice   Plan transactions and events   Build functional objects

Acknowledgments

Sue J. Kim designed this book and created the illustrations. I can't imagine a better collaborator. Sue is the complete professional. Creativity, precision, technical ability, thoughtfulness, responsiveness, drive, an open mind but a firm point of view... Sue has it all. She is a great model (including for us lawyers) on how to learn about a client's goals, develop a framework, create a plan, bring ideas to the table, do outstanding technical work, and get the deal closed. I am deeply admiring of, and grateful for, her work.

Mei Li, a 2015 graduate of Stanford Law School and now a lawyer at a major firm in Silicon Valley, collaborated with me in developing the prototype for the book. Mei brought imagination, energy, care, and design talent, as well as an invaluable soon-to-be-an-associate perspective, to her editorial, design, and technical work on the prototype. She was essential to the launch of the project, and I'm thankful for her work and colleagueship.

Jordan Bowler, Erin Cho, Andrew Hall, Melissa Magner, and David Moore, all former students in the Organizations and Transactions Clinic at Stanford Law School, read the entire manuscript and, entirely in line with what I observed of their work in the clinic, gave me wonderfully helpful criticisms and suggestions. They pushed me pretty hard, and always in a good direction.

Eva Gutierrez, a former teaching fellow in the clinic, reviewed the entire manuscript. Eva gave me great (real world) ideas based on her experiences working in major firms, teaching in the clinic, and now practicing as an in-house lawyer at a data analytics company.

My faculty colleague George Fisher generously reviewed the chapter on litigation, for which I'm fortunate and grateful. Faculty colleagues Juliet Brodie, Paul Goldstein, Bill Koski, Phil Malone, and George Triantis, clinic client Sean Hewens, clinic colleagues Brenda Munoz and Michelle Sonu, and former students Rachael Apfel, Phillip Arredondo, Jocelyn Dicker, Sara Gates, Brent Harris, Mansi Kothari, Devon Mobley-Ritter, Cameron Ormsby, Richard Sapien, Eric Silverberg, Ryan Stouffer, and Kaleisha Stuart, all provided guidance and encouragement along the way.

I am indebted to the remarkable reference staff at the Robert Crown Law Library at Stanford Law School for their consistent creativity, diligence, and responsiveness. They have to be the best in the business.

I wish to thank Adam Rosman and Elizabeth Flisser Rosman for their generous support of work at Stanford on the use of visual communication in legal practice.

Finally, I'm thankful for the clients I've had the good fortune to represent over the years, the colleagues in the firms and businesses where I've worked, my colleagues at Stanford, and the students and guests that have come through the clinic. Together they've provided the opportunities to draw pictures, layer on the layers, do the documents, and generally reflect on how to help new lawyers get their hands around the practice, and how to produce quality work for clients. Good folks, and good fun.

Permissions

Page 14 Sketching and Lawyers

Roam quote from Dan Roam, *The Back of the Napkin: Selling Ideas and Solving Problems Through Pictures* 3-4, copyright ©2008 by Digital Roam, Inc. Reprinted by permission of Portfolio, an imprint of Penguin Publishing Group, a division of Penguin Random House LLC.

Conboy quote from Kevin Conboy, "Diagramming Transactions: Some Modest Proposals and a Few Suggested Rules," 16 *Transactions: The Tenn. J. Bus. L.* 91 (2014). http://trace.tennessee,edu/transactions/vol16/iss1/5/. Reprinted by permission of Trace: Tennessee Research and Creative Exchange ©2015.

Weise quote from Steve Weise, "Get Your Crayons Out," 8 *Bus. L. Today* 1 (1999), available at: http://apps.americanbar.org/buslaw/blt/8-5crayons.html. Reprinted by permission of the American Bar Association, permission conveyed through Copyright Clearance Center, Inc., and by the author.

Page 15 Thinking

Suwa and Tversky quote from Masaki Suwa and Barbara Tversky, "External Representations Contribute to the Dynamic Construction of Ideas," *Diagrams 2002 – Diagrammatic Representation and Inference – Second International Conference* 342 (2002) (Mary Hegarty, et. al., eds.) Reprinted by kind permission of Springer Science+Business Media, and by the author.

Heiser, Tversky, and Silverman quote from Julie Heiser, Barbara Tversky, and Mia Silverman, "Sketches for and from Collaboration," *Visual and Spatial Reasoning in Design III* 69 (2004) (J. Gero, B. Tversky, and T. Knight, eds.). Reprinted by permission of the Design Lab at the University of Sydney, and by the author.

Page 16 Discussion Partner

Laseau quote from Paul Laseau, *Graphic Thinking for Architects & Designers* 8 (3d ed.) (2001). Reprinted by permission of John Wiley & Sons, Inc., permission conveyed through Copyright Clearance Center, Inc.

Dubovsky and Dee quotes from *Drawing/Thinking: Confronting an Electronic Age* 72, 66 (2008) (Mark Treib, ed.). Reprinted by permission of Routledge, permission conveyed through Copyright Clearance Center, Inc.

Page 17 Collaboration

Heiser, Tversky, and Silverman quote from Julie Heiser, Barbara Tversky, and Mia Silverman, "Sketches for and from Collaboration," *Visual and Spatial Reasoning in Design III* 77 (2004) (J. Gero, B. Tversky, and T. Knight, eds.). Reprinted by permission of the Design Lab at the University of Sydney, and by the author.

Craft and Cairns quote from Brook Craft and Paul Cairns, "Using Sketching to Aid the Collaborative Design of Information Visualisation Software – A Case Study," *Human Work Interaction Design: Designing for Human Work* 108 (2006) (Torkil Clemmensen, et. al., eds.) Reprinted by kind permission of Springer Science+Business Media, and by the author.

Page 18 Seeing the Big Picture

Dubovsky quote from *Drawing/Thinking: Confronting an Electronic Age* 72 (2008) (Mark Treib, ed.). Reprinted by permission of Routledge, permission conveyed through Copyright Clearance Center, Inc.

Porter quote from Elizabeth G. Porter, "Taking Images Seriously," 114 *Colum. L. Rev.* 1687, 1753 (2014). Reprinted by permission of the Columbia Law Review, permission conveyed directly and through Copyright Clearance Center, Inc., and by the author.

Rosman quote from Adam L. Rosman, "Visualizing the Law: Using Charts, Diagrams, and Other Images to Improve Legal Briefs," 63 *J. Legal Educ.* 70 (2013), copyright © 2013 American Association of Law Schools. Reprinted by permission of the American Association of Law Schools, and by the author.

Page 19 Pictures in the Head

Weise quotes from Steve Weise, "Get Your Crayons Out," 8 *Bus. L. Today* 1 (1999), available at: http://apps.americanbar.org/buslaw/blt/8-5crayons.html. Reprinted by permission of the American Bar Association, permission conveyed through Copyright Clearance Center, Inc., and by the author.

Porter quote from Elizabeth G. Porter, "Taking Images Seriously," 114 *Colum. L. Rev.* 1687, 1753 (2014), Reprinted by permission of the Columbia Law Review, permission conveyed directly and through Copyright Clearance Center, Inc., and by the author.

Page 20 Learning Styles and Physicality

Barron and Dubovsky quotes from *Drawing/Thinking: Confronting an Electronic Age* 115, 75 (2008) (Mark Treib, ed.). Reprinted by permission of Routledge, permission conveyed through Copyright Clearance Center, Inc.

Page 21 You Don't Have to be an Artist

Brewer quote from Joshua Brewer, "Sketch, Sketch, Sketch," *52 Weeks of UX* (blog post), http://52weeksofux.com/post/346650933/sketch-sketch-sketch. Reprinted by permission of the author.

Santa Maria quote from Jason Santa Maria, "Pretty Sketchy" (blog post), http://v4.jasonsantamaria.com/articles/pretty-sketchy/ Reprinted by permission of the author.

Sources

Transactional Legal Work

Alicia Alvarez and Paul R. Tremblay, *Introduction to Transactional Lawyering Practice* (2013)

George W. Dent, Jr., "Business Lawyers as Enterprise Architects," 64 *Bus. Law.* 279 (2009)

Ronald J. Gilson, "Value Creation by Business Lawyers: Legal Skills and Asset Pricing," 94 *Yale L. J.* 239 (1984)

David Howarth, *Law as Engineering: Thinking about What Lawyers Do* (2013)

Daniel Lee and Matt Swarz, *The Corporate, Securities, and M&A Lawyer's Job: A Survival Guide* (2007)

Richard K. Neuman, Jr., *Transactional Lawyering Skills: Client Interviewing, Counseling, and Negotiation* (2012)

Karl S. Okamoto, "Teaching Transactional Lawyering," 1 *Drexel L. Rev.* 69 (2009)

Karl S. Okamoto, "Reputation and the Value of Lawyers," 74 *Ore. L. Rev.* 15 (1995)

Elizabeth Pollman, "Value Creation by Business Lawyers: Where Are We and Where Are We Going?," 15 *U.C. Davis Bus. L. J.* 13 (2014)

Steven L. Schwarcz, "Explaining the Value of Transactional Lawyering," 12 *Stan. J. L. Bus. & Fin.* 486 (2006)

Visuals, Thinking, and Communication

Robert Ambrogi, "Vision Quest: Visual Law Services are Worth a Thousand Words — and Big Money," 100 *A.B.A. J.* 34 (2014)

Errol Barron, "Drawing in the Digital Age," *Drawing/Thinking: Confronting an Electronic Age* (2008) (Mark Treib, ed.)

Joshua Brewer, "Sketch, Sketch, Sketch," *52 Weeks of UX* (blog post), http://52weeksofux.com/post/346650933/sketch-sketch-sketch

Kevin Conboy, "Diagramming Transactions: Some Modest Proposals and a Few Suggested Rules," 16 *Transactions: Tenn. J. Bus. L.* 91 (2014), http://trace.tennessee,edu/transactions/vol16/iss1/5/

Brook Craft and Paul Cairns, "Using Sketching to Aid the Collaborative Design of Information Visualisation Software – A Case Study," *Human Work Interaction Design: Designing for Human Work* (2006) (Torkil Clemmensen, et. al., eds.)

Catherine Dee, "Plus and Minus: Critical Drawing for Landscape Design," *Drawing/Thinking: Confronting an Electronic Age* (2008) (Mark Treib, ed.)

Ellen Yi-Luen Do and Mark D. Gross, "Thinking with Diagrams in Architectural Design," *Artificial Intelligence Review* 15: 135 (1999)

Anthony Dubovsky, "The Euphoria of the Everyday," *Drawing/Thinking: Confronting an Electronic Age* 72 (2008) (Mark Treib, ed.)

Neal Feigenson and Christina Spiesel, *Law on Display: The Digital Transformation of Legal Persuasion and Judgment* (2009)

Eugene S. Ferguson, *Engineering and the Mind's Eye* (1994)

Doug Fitch, "Drawing from Design," *Thinking Through Drawing: Practice into Knowledge* (2011) (Andrea Kantrowitz, Angela Brew and Michelle Fava, eds.)

Felice C. Frankel and Angela H. DePace, *Visual Strategies: A Practical Guide to Graphics for Scientists & Engineers* (2012)

Julie Heiser, Barbara Tversky, and Mia Silverman, "Sketches for and from Collaboration," *Visual and Spatial Reasoning in Design III* (2004) (J. Gero, B. Tversky, and T. Knight, eds.)

Steve Johansen and Ruth Anne Robbins, "Art-iculating the Analysis: Systemizing the Decision to Use Visuals as Legal Reasoning," 20 *Legal Writing* 57 (2015)

Paul Laseau, *Graphic Thinking for Architects & Designers* (3d ed.) (2001)

Remko van der Lugt, "How Sketching Can Affect the Idea Generation Process in Design Group Meetings," *Design Studies*, Vol. 26(2), 101 (2005)

Jason Santa Maria, "Pretty Sketchy" (blog post), http://v4.jasonsantamaria.com/articles/pretty-sketchy/

Felicia L. McKoy et al., "Influence of Design Representation on Effectiveness of Idea Generation," *Proceedings of the ASME Design Engineering Technical Conference*, Vol. 4 39 (2001)

Michael D. Murray, "Leaping Language and Cultural Barriers with Visual Legal Rhetoric," 49 *U.S.F. L. Rev.* 61 (2015) (Law Review Forum)

Elizabeth G. Porter, "Taking Images Seriously," 114 *Colum. L. Rev.* 1687 (2014)

Dan Roam, *The Back of the Napkin: Selling Ideas and Solving Problems Through Pictures* (2013)

Adam L. Rosman, "Visualizing the Law: Using Charts, Diagrams, and Other Images to Improve Legal Briefs," 63 *J. Legal Educ.* 70 (2013)

Brett G. Scharffs, "Law as Craft," 54 *Vand. L. Rev.* 2245 (2001)

Robert Sennett, *The Craftsman* (2008)

Masaki Suwa and Barbara Tversky, "External Representations Contribute to the Dynamic Construction of Ideas," *Diagrams 2002 — Diagrammatic Representation and Inference — Second International Conference* (2002) (Mary Hegarty, et. al., eds.)

Rebecca Tushnet, "Worth a Thousand Words: The Images of Copyright," 125 *Harv. L. Rev.* 683 (2012)

Barbara Tversky, "Obsessed by Lines," *Thinking Through Drawing: Practice into Knowledge* (2011) (Andrea Kantrowitz, Angela Brew and Michelle Fava, eds.)

Barbara Tversky, "What do Sketches Say about Thinking?," *Sketch Understanding: Papers from the AAAI Spring Symposium* (2002) (Randall Davis et. al., eds.)

Steve Weise, "Get Your Crayons Out," 8 *Bus. L. Today* (1999), available at: http://apps.americanbar.org/buslaw/blt/8-5crayons.html

Touch, Motion, and Learning

Marieke Longcamp, et al., "Learning Through Hand- or Typewriting Influences Visual Recognition of New Graphic Shapes: Behavioral and Functional Imaging Evidence," 20.5 *Journal of Cognitive Neuroscience* 802 (2008)

Anne Mangen and Jean-Luc Velay, "Digitizing Literacy: Reflections on the Haptics of Writing," *Advances in Haptics* (2010) (Mehrdad Hosseini Zadeh, ed.)

Anna Mikulak, "Getting it in Writing: Writing the Old-Fashioned Way May Enhance Learning and Memory," 27 *Observer, Association for Psychological Science* (2014)

Legal Reading

Linda L. Berger, "Applying New Rhetoric to Legal Discourse: The Ebb and Flow of Reader and Writer, Text and Content," 49 *J. Legal Educ.* 155 (1999)

Scott J. Burnham, "How to Read a Contract," 45 *Ariz. L. Rev.* 133 (2003)

Scott J. Burnham, "Critical Reading of Contracts," 23 *Legal. Stud. F.* 391 (1991)

Leah M. Christensen, "Legal Reading and Success in Law School: An Empirical Study," 30 *Seattle U. L. Rev.* 603 (2006)

Dorothy H. Deegan, "Exploring Individual Differences among Novices Reading in a Specific Domain: The Case of Law," 30 *Reading Res. Q.* 154 (1995)

Peter Dewitz, "Reading Law: Three Suggestions for Legal Education," 27 *U. Tol. L. Rev.* 657 (1999)

Peter Dewitz, "Legal Education: A Problem of Learning from Text," 23 *N.Y.U. Rev. L. & Soc. Change* 225 (1997)

Dorothy H. Evensen, et al., "Law School Admission Council Grants Report 08-02, Developing an Assessment of First-Year Law Students' Critical Case Reading and Reasoning Ability: Phase 2" (2008), available at http://www.lsacnet.org/LSACResources/Research/GR/GR-08-02.pdf.

Mary A. Lundberg, "Metacognitive Aspects of Reading Comprehension: Studying Understanding in Legal Case Analysis," 22 *Reading Res. Q.* 407 (1987)

Ruth Ann McKinney, *Reading Like a Lawyer: Time-Saving Strategies for Reading Law Like an Expert* (2005)

Jay A. Mitchell, "Reading (in the Clinic) is Fundamental," 19 *Clinical L. Rev.* 297 (2012)

Laurel Currie Oates, "Leveling the Playing Field: Helping Students Succeed by Helping Them Learn to Read as Expert Lawyers," 80 *St. John's L. Rev.* 227 (2006)

Contracts and Other Legal Documents

Ronald J. Gilson, Charles F. Sabel, and Robert E. Scott, "Braiding: The Interaction of Formal and Informal Contracting in Theory, Practice, and Doctrine," 110 *Colum. L. Rev.* 1377 (2010)

Mitu Gulati and Robert E. Scott, *The Three and a Half Minute Transaction: Boilerplate and the Limits of Contract Design* (2012)

Jay A. Mitchell, "Document appreciation: some characteristics of legal documents (and talking with students about them)," http://papers.ssrn.com/sol3/papers.cfm?abstract_id=2406047 (2014)

Jay A. Mitchell, "Putting Some Product into Work-Product: Corporate Lawyers Learning from Designers," 12 *Berkeley Bus. L. J.* 1 (2015)

George C. Triantis, "Improving Contract Quality: Modularity, Technology, and Innovation in Contract Design," 18 *Stan. J. L. Bus. & Fin.* 177 (2013)

Professional Responsibility

American Bar Association, *Model Rules of Prof'l Conduct* (2015)

Michael A. Pittenger, et. al., "M&A Deal Counsel's Role in Creating a Winning Written Record for Defending Breach of Fiduciary Duty Litigation" (2013), http://www.potteranderson.com/media/publication/583_M_A_20Deal_20Counsel_27s_20Role_20in_20Creating_20a_20Winning_20Written_20Record_20for_20Defending_20Breach_20of_20Fiduciary_20Duty_20Litigation_20MAP_20JMS_20Apr_202013.pdf

Report and Recommendations of the Committee on Lawyer Business Ethics of the ABA Section of Business, "The Lawyer as Director of A Client," 57 *Bus. Law.* 387 (2001)

Robert Salerno, "Sharing Privileged Information During Due Diligence" (2013), http://media.mofo.com/files/Uploads/Images/131206-Sharing-Privileged-Information-During-Due-Diligence.pdf

A Note about the Sources

This listing reflects an emphasis on works relating to transactional practice generally, works concerning topics addressed in the book but not typically the subject of overt law school or continuing education instruction (such as visual thinking and legal reading), and works that provide useful perspectives on contracts, board minutes, diligence, and other everyday aspects of corporate practice.

About the Author

Jay A. Mitchell is Professor of Law and Director of the Organizations and Transactions Clinic at Stanford Law School. Before joining the law school in 2007, Mitchell was chief corporate counsel at Levi Strauss & Co. for many years, a partner and associate at the Heller Ehrman firm in San Francisco, and an associate at Arnold & Porter in Washington, D.C. He is a graduate of Stanford University and the University of Virginia School of Law.